A FRIEND CALLED
CALLED
Process

Published in Nigeria by WORITAL GLOBAL, 2023
6b Lanre Awolokun Street, Gbagada Phase 2, Lagos, Nigeria.
WORITAL (hello@worital.com)
+2348114027024

Cover Design, Interior Layout, Print and Bound by:
WORITAL (hello@worital.com)

FOREWORD

Not only are we a creature of habits; we are individuals packaged with gifts and talents to create, as well as add sustainable values to the society. The truth that I have discovered in my journey to significance, especially as a leader in the marketplace is that you can succeed if you are guided by relevant principles and an undying willingness to submit to an uncompromising friend called – PROCESS.

Allow me to share a few principles that I have learned about the inevitable path of the process required for anyone who desires to develop and display a better version of themselves; or anyone who craves to add value at any level. In no special order, I have learned that process is what brings out the best of anything valuable. For example, grapefruits are better utilized when processed and allowed to ferment over a period that produces some of the finest wine. So, after a given time the grapefruit attains a level of mastery possible because it was processed through time.

Therefore, anyone; including you and I can equally attain a level of self-mastery depending on the level of patience we are willing to exercise through the process of self-awareness. This is the only way any human being can fulfil his/her purpose in life, calling, or vocation. Another important lesson I have learned is that process increases the value of anything of worth. A person's purpose is not some flimsy talk of calling or assignment; your life purpose is a worthy call to serve a fellow human being not necessarily for gain or profit. However, its worthiness only increases through self-development and focus.

Being an entrepreneur in the product and service delivery business for many years has taught me the essential part of the process in the production cycle of a product or service. The proper processing of a product or service gives an exchangeable value to its worth. As a person of worth, the acceptance of various processes allows for optimum value to be achieved.

In this book, brilliantly written by my good friend Ola Olaleye, you will be challenged through a systemic approach to reconsider the way you have viewed the processes we all must face and embrace in our journey to success and significance. The author pushes the reader, to go after newer concepts, ideas, and knowledge as effective tools to leverage processes to our advantage. Also,

'A friend called process' does not leave readers to themselves to figure out how to overcome life barriers that can negatively impact the process of achieving fulfilment in life.

Ola Olaleye, you, and I have witnessed the transformational power in consistency, and I love the fact that you didn't leave this important component out of this masterpiece because it is a critical ingredient, to being an achiever and a highly successful individual. A lot of dreamers quit too soon and abandon their dreams as well as promises to be a source of hope and inspiration to members of their community or even their workplace. Thank you for setting the standard high through your own life and work; it is not a wonder why you have received several prestigious recognition awards and I have no doubts that there are more to come shortly.

This book has come at a time I believe it is most needed because it will not only provide a guide for us to attain a better version of ourselves; it is also loaded with encouragement for those who are struggling with their identity. It serves as a guide urging them to move forward with self-belief, tenacity and audacity. Thank you, my dear friend, Ola for your commitment to excellence and generosity and I also thank you for the opportunity which you wrote extensively on in this book and have presented to me to write these opening words. I certainly do not take this for granted – THANK YOU!

Now, you go and sell millions and millions of copies of this incredible life and purpose handbook. Your effort has surely paid off like your other projects. Well done!!! God bless you, Amen.

Femi Adun
CEO & Co-Founder, PactLeadership USA

CONTENTS

INTRODUCTION

An overnight success! Have you had someone refer to you as one? Or perhaps, you have referred to someone as such? Many times, we use this expression to describe success that we cannot explain. We assume the person simply wrote one book and became successful. We assume they struck one business deal, and voila! Now, they are rich. We take no account of the years of toiling and many failures, the dark nights with thoughts of throwing in the towel. We have no inkling as to how many times they started a business and had to shut it down. The many creditors they might have had to hide from or renegotiate payment terms with. The strain on relationships, the self-doubt, the anxiety as they feared that yet again another attempt might come to nothing.

We often define success in terms of material acquisition but success goes beyond the financial reward that comes from working hard. It includes the impact that we make in the lives of the people who encounter us or our businesses. Being successful means mastering one's craft, and being able to build a framework that can be taught to others.

The price to pay for success is huge but attainable. Becoming successful is not for the faint-hearted. It is for people who want to do more than test the waters. It is for those who want to give their all or nothing. It is for those who want to jump with both feet in. It is for those who have burned the boats, yet, must return home. It is for people who are afraid, yet, go ahead to do it!

It is for people who know they must put in the work whether they feel like it or not. They know they can take a break, but they must not stop. They know they can change the strategy, but the goal remains unchanged. They know they must keep moving even if it means that they crawl, whilst keeping their eye on the goal. Being successful means refusing to take 'No' for an answer.

A friend called Process is a collection of tested and proven principles that I have used to build and grow my business. In the last thirteen years, I have successfully started a charity and built a coaching business. My charity organisation, through our various platforms, has transformed over 5000 lives. The charity is also a nominee for the Queen's Award for Voluntary Service 2021. In June 2022, I was invited to attend the Queen's Garde party in the capacity of charity head.

Beyond fate or prayers, it takes several processes and lots of work – hard work, if you will achieve this feat. Being a person of

Christian faith, I believe there are serendipitous events that give a boost to our businesses. Chance meetings and opportunities that we cannot explain often happen, but I know for a fact that serendipity alone cannot and will not make you a successful person. You must consciously follow proven procedures, otherwise called processes to achieve your business goals.

It is my aim that this book will bring much-needed knowledge to those seeking to understand the process of becoming successful in any sphere of life. It contains personal stories to illustrate the principles. I desire that the process will become clear and that myths about what it takes to be successful will be unraveled.

The successes we record in our businesses or personal dealings usually do not result from mere coincidence. Although there is the possibility to experience a 'one-off' victory without much input, however, for it to be consistent and sustainable, we must put in the work. 'When the rain falls on fertile ground, it wets it and makes its seeds bud.' From this quote, it is clear that there is first – a fertile ground, and second – seeds, before any budding can occur.

Similarly, the vision and goals you aim for your business will not just materialise until you consistently follow processes and take action towards achieving those goals. This is exactly what becoming successful is like, it is a process. A Friend Called Process is my attempt to help people see that they do not have to be extraordinary to succeed and that they already have everything needed to make the transition from where they are to where they desire to be.

I look back on my journey and I realize that everyone who desires to be more and do more, can achieve their dream.

This book is for everyone who feels a sense of unease in their lives even though they may be considered successful.

It is for those who have big dreams but fear taking that first step.

It is for those who have been told, they cannot do it because it has never been done!

It is for those who are constantly doubting themselves and hiding behind the scenes when they really should be in the frontlines.

It is for anyone who wants to make a difference!

Welcome, as we embark on the journey to extraordinariness!

CHAPTER ONE

Finding Your Purpose

At the core of being successful in life is knowing what your mission on earth is. One of the easiest ways to become disillusioned with life is to think that life is about the mundane, the trappings of success and the power; so, when we feel like we do not measure up to these standards, we begin to feel like we are wasting life or like our lives do not count. And while being successful comes with these trappings, who we have become turns out to be more important than what we have acquired.

Who we are is so important because if we lose everything we have, the person who created the successful life still lives within us. The ability to recreate the life we want even when it had been lost is tied to our life's purpose.

1

Your purpose and mission are places that you can only arrive at by peeling layers off and taking a chance on becoming a newer version of yourself.

We are constantly telling people to be themselves, and while that is a good piece of advice, sometimes, who or what you are will not be sufficient to bring the magnitude of the task you have at hand to life. There are people, who by virtue of being born in certain countries, are already at a disadvantage in life. Based on this, their mindset and beliefs might be limiting, unless they make efforts to gain new skills and receive new insights, whilst learning new ways of doing things. No matter how passionate they are about making an impact or being successful, it will be a tall order to get from where they are to where they know they should or could be; telling people 'be yourself' in this situation might be an unhelpful piece of advice.

It is possible to think that life is all about going to school and getting a high-paying job, perhaps getting married and even raising kids, and buying a big house that we pay for, for most of our lives and while I do not denigrate anyone who has chosen to live this life or who feels restricted and unable to break out of this mould... well, newsflash – there is more to life than the rat race. A friend of mine shared her ordeal with working in the bank.

Her quest for purpose started when she witnessed ex-bankers come back to collect their pensions; many of them had lost their glow and did not resemble people who had any experience of the corporate world. They had little or no savings. The best of them, in many cases, had managed to secure a mortgage which is the house they live in and for which they were thankful, but once the bank job was gone, they had nothing else to do.

A good number of them had put in 25 years or more, and in the twilight of their lives, had nothing to look forward to.

In my birth country, stories abound of countless pensioners, who after putting in as many as 35 years, now have to fight for pensions which sometimes are not paid for several months. Yet, these people believed at one time that all they had to do was get a government job which could guarantee a level of career security, and earn them pensions.

Your life's purpose is your ticket out of mediocrity and dissatisfaction. It is your ticket to taking hold of life and living it on your own terms. When you know what you are meant to be doing, who you are meant to become, where you are meant to be... you are freed from the burden of living up to other people's expectations of you, as well as having the joy of knowing you are on a mission to impact lives positively.

You might be thinking and perhaps feeling overwhelmed because I have just stirred you up for something you are not quite ready for, you might also be feeling triggered right now because it might sound like I am saying you are not doing enough. However, this is not my intention at all . What I am trying to do is to get you to look inwards and ask yourself if this is all there is to you and if you are happy with who you are and where you are.

If you are content with who and where you are, then maybe this book is not for you but if you have been feeling unsettled for a while now, if you have been struggling with an internal conflict, if you suddenly feel like you are made for more yet do not know where to start, if you have been feeling like the essence of who you are is trapped beneath the facade that people see and you want out…then you are the one, this book has been written for.

Eighteen years ago, I decided to relocate to the United Kingdom from Nigeria. I had a strong perception that I could be more, but there was so much holding me back those years, and I needed to break the mould. Regardless of how much work I put in, I was unable to make an impact on a scale that I would have loved to. Somehow, the opportunity for relocation came, and I knew the United Kingdom would give me that platform for expression, hence, I became intentional about my decision to relocate.

Now you might be asking, 'How do I find my life's purpose?' and 'Does everyone have a specific life purpose?'

Permit me to answer these questions by giving you questions of my own to ponder on:

- Do you feel an unease every time you imagine your life remaining the way it is, even though you consider yourself successful?

- Do you feel like you should be doing more but you are currently stuck?
- Are you often unhappy but cannot trace the source of your unhappiness?
- Do you find yourself having great opportunities at work but never being able to make the best of them?
- Are you suddenly tired of things you used to enjoy?
- Do you find yourself searching for the meaning of life?
- Have you perhaps never given purpose discovery a thought because you are so enmeshed in the rat race and simply on autopilot?

If you answered yes to even one of these questions, it means there is more that you desire from life, and you need to become more curious about how to discover this.

Now that you have identified a possibility of a certain specific life purpose, allow me to backtrack to the first question – How do I find my life's purpose?

To manage this process, I will share what I call *pointers to purpose:*

a) Intuition… You will know!
Most times, we know what we should be doing but we are afraid to step out because of what people might say. We may feel incompetent and overwhelmed by the process, hence, deciding to play small. When I decided to start The Esther's Company, it was based on my knowledge that I had to impact the black community in the UK, where I live. Like most people, I had

limiting thoughts; I was worried about what people would say and if my vision would be accepted.

However, the knowledge that 'this' is what I ought to be doing, gave me the courage to forge ahead. So, please listen to your inner voice. We must understand that our inner voice is quiet, it almost feels like it does not want to have to reach too hard, so you really need to be sensitive to it. If you always have to argue with yourself, you need to stop and ask, 'Why does this thought bother me so much?'

b) What do you feel drawn to?

Another pointer to your life's purpose may be what you are naturally drawn to? You may have a crisp and clear voice. People might say, 'Oh! You should really be singing', however, you may feel drawn to use your voice for animation recordings or voice-overs instead of singing. You may enjoy storytelling, the voice inflection and the joy it brings to children or your listeners. You may feel drawn to broadcasting. My friend who I mentioned earlier who worked in the bank had told me she felt drawn to teach but as a young adult whose friends were getting bank jobs (bank jobs were very prestigious then when I lived in Nigeria), how could she just decide she wanted to teach? So, she also got a bank job and for the 5 years she was with the bank, she felt very miserable. Guess what she is doing now? Yes, she is teaching! When you feel drawn to a vocation, that could be a pointer to what your life's purpose might be and a sure way to being successful in life.

c) What gives you immense joy?

When you find yourself doing an activity that you enjoy so much that time passes while you are at it and you do not even realise it, that could be a pointer to your purpose. If you find yourself carrying out certain jobs for people before you have even discussed payment, that may be an indication of what your life's purpose is. You see, when you set out on a mission to become a person of impact and to be successful, you will encounter difficulties that will make you want to throw in the towel; however, reminding yourself why you started and having joy in what you do, are usually the two things that would keep you going.

d) What causes you pain?

Do you find yourself trying to protect people from the pain you have experienced? Do you discover that you are giving relationship tips and advice based on positive or negative experiences? Do you see yourself pushing others to do more because you wish someone had done the same for you in the past? If you find out a couple of these apply to you, your life's purpose might be coaching. You then need to identify the specific area(s) you feel capable to support people.

In the past, I struggled to merge my faith with my authentic life. I assumed I had to be a certain way as a true Christian (believer), which made me erroneously believe I could not be my authentic self; however, I came to understand that, to be who or what I was meant to be, I had to be able to merge my personality with my faith. This was because I had to accept where I was on my journey of faith and not beat myself too much for not being the super person that others wanted me to be. Having found this freedom, I can now teach people to become the most authentic versions of themselves.

e) Pay attention to your strengths

Your strengths are often pointers to what you should be doing in life though not always. Let me explain. If you were raised in a dysfunctional home, for instance, you may have the desire to see families function well. As a person, you may not have experienced a functional home, but your passion, fueled by your pain, can give you the enablement to find purpose – through helping families heal from dysfunction or helping families function properly.

You will find yourself learning new skills and using the new strength gained to help people. If you have the ability to make complex concepts easy, you may find that strength purposeful for working with children. So again, look to your strengths, your gifts and talents to see how they lead you to your life's purpose.

You may also consider taking professional personality tests to determine other not-so obvious strengths.

f) What are your values?

Many people think, to prosper in life, they must throw their values away. This is not true! If you find yourself compromising on your integrity to succeed, then you are as far from your life's purpose as you can be. Your values are pointers to what you should be doing in life. Success is not necessarily measured in monetary acquisition. While being successful could includes money, you must have a more definitive objective on what actual success means to you, beyond monetary quantification.

However, whether the success you seek is monetary or not, your values will always guide you on what you should be doing. When you have to decide on which direction to go; your values can serve as a map to guide you. There are certain vocations or careers you would not even bother with simply because they violate who you are at your core. Do keep your values, they will point you to your life's purpose.

Finding our purpose can feel like a daunting task. Often, we want to see the whole picture, we want to see the little steps and the outcomes along the way, without ever fully knowing what we may encounter. Just take that first step or what you might call, 'a leap of faith.' If we set out to understand how everything might unfold before we begin, we may never start the journey of being successful.

At this juncture, it is important to mention that every experience we go through, somewhat points to our purpose. For some, this may easily become a trigger, especially if you have to unearth memories of how you arrived at choosing these values. In every situation, good or bad, there is a lesson and an opportunity. What opportunity has your situation presented?

Do you know a person who has, or have you made bad investment decisions and lost a lot of money? Or probably, you have had a financial setback in the past? Could this motivate you to learn financial skills and help others to avoid this pitfall by using your experience to teach people better financial management? Possibly, you have experienced loss? Could that experience help others who might be suffering or grieving? Loss and grief are extremely difficult to deal with or recover from. When we grieve a loved one, we are honoring the relationship that has now ended. There could be a chance here, to help others go through their grief in such a way that it doesn't consume them.

Think it out loud

It is common to hear people give advice like, *'Why don't you try that business? Such and such a person started it and now they have made it.'* Even though these individuals mean well, it is clear that many people are walking blind and without a sense of who they are, what they want or where they are headed. Decisions appear to be made based on what others have done, rather than on their innate gifts, personalities and peculiar experiences. Don't fold, take the opportunities life hands you and become a person of significance.

To become successful, we cannot be like everyone or do what everyone is doing. Therein, lies the frustration we feel and this could create a raging conflict within us. We must find our purpose, and identify with everything that is unique to us – nothing must be wasted; our pain, shame, gifts, skills, education, family background, life experiences (good or bad), personality, network... Everything is purposeful to our existence, consequently, to our success.

Task

To help you identify what you might be called to do;

1. List 5 things you enjoy doing.
2. List 5 things you can do effortlessly.
3. What in life makes you angry that you wish to change?
4. What are you so passionate about that you can do without being paid?
5. Which of all of these can you do without losing a sense of who you are?

CHAPTER TWO

Authenticity: Wear Your Gifts on Your Sleeves.

Have you ever met someone whom you thought was trying too hard to be `seen and heard'? They otherwise may have been a perfect host/hostess or conversationalist. Sadly, they are too caught up in playing to the gallery to live out their best. In the same way, you may have heard people say things like, 'This is who I am, take it or leave it' but are then quick to get upset when you decide not to 'take it.'

Being authentic is a must! To be truly successful, you must not only have, but show quality. Authenticity is the quality of being original. There is no room for less; it is what makes people trust you. We become authentic when we become aware of who we are in our totality. Sometimes we mistake people who are being rude to be real. We say, 'He always speaks his mind, he doesn't care whose ox is gored… he is so real.' Well, that is not necessarily the case!

To thine own self be true… Know yourself, know your worth and present your authentic self to your purpose.

Borrowing the words of the thespian legend, William Shakespeare, 'To become or maintain one's authentic self, you must know yourself.' You cannot be an original if you do not know who you are. Many of our struggles with accepting and showcasing our authentic selves emanate from our childhood.

Some of us were raised to be over-functioning over-performers. Maybe, the only time you got approval was when you did something good or phenomenal. For a lot of us, achieving success in school was our way of performing so we could be loved and accepted by our parents. For others, hiding our true selves and becoming who others wanted us to be was our way of gaining acceptance; being the mature child and the perfect child might have been our way of being 'seen' in the family. Possibly, our siblings were asked to be more like us; with this, we learnt that to be accepted, we had to be a certain way.

Perhaps in school, children who behaved a certain way always got into trouble, so we learned to hide those tendencies if we had them.

Like any habit, once you adopt a certain way of 'be-ing', it becomes who you are. And in a few years, this façade, which was meant to save you from the ridicule and criticism of your parents, teachers or peers, now becomes the persona you use in interacting with the world, to the extent that you forget who you really are. Thus, let your talent show and make it shine!

When we are not our authentic selves and we attempt to do big things, we will struggle. You will probably disagree with me, but remember success is beyond the laurels you have acquired, the money you have made, the big house, fancy car or schools your children attend. Being successful is the impact you are making on others, without losing yourself in the process. If I lose my health, values or close relationships in my quest to be successful, then my success cannot be said to be complete even if I have the trappings of success. My ability to see how my actions are impacting others and my humility to make necessary adjustments are what make me successful.

If your mental health is impacted negatively or your relationships are in turmoil; perhaps you did not have time to spend with your children as you pursued your career, now that you are at the peak, they would not even speak to you, are you truly successful?

It is important to note that being authentic is not all cheery. One of the reasons people are afraid to put themselves out there is the fear of being abandoned. They fear they will not be accepted; they have all their lives performed for people's acceptance, and they do not know any other way to live. In fact, asking them to be more adventurous or to be less fearful could lead to them keeping their distance from you. You may be accused of being a know-it-all, a bully, too critical or pushy. Not everyone is going to appreciate you leaving your comfort zone and pushing for more of your abilities and capabilities.

Bear in mind that not everyone will be comfortable with your new upgrade. You are now a person who is stepping up, becoming more daring and successful, hence, it is bound to make certain people uncomfortable because it forces them to face the fact that they may be living a lie. You force them to see it doesn't take a genius to live out success, it takes a doer... and no one wants to feel that exposed. So yes, being authentic may not keep your old circle but guess what, it will birth a new, more supportive and empowering tribe.

Authenticity: Success, Service and Empathy

Authenticity is such a key element to being successful because:

At the core of authenticity is self-awareness, self-acceptance and self-deployment: This means you know who you are – strengths, weaknesses, beliefs, values, motivations, emotions, and threats – to top it, you even know how others view you. Sometimes, we may know who we are but may be lacking in knowing how others view us, which may cause us to make poor choices in relationships – friendships or professions, alike. So now you not only know yourself, you accept yourself – warts and all!

16

You accept that your experiences, both good and bad, have formed the person that you are. You accept that there was a time you did not do well but it was only because you did not know better; now you do and hence, you will do better. You begin to gradually break away from the usual workplace apathy that is associated with success and apply the role of empathy to the destination called success. Success doesn't have to be brutal.

Having understood this, give yourself the joy of embracing your person. Self-acceptance is one of the greatest acts of service you can do for yourself. No matter how kind people are to you, if you do not accept yourself, not only will you not thrive, you will also find it hard to be someone who allows others to thrive. Have you noticed that some of the most admired corporate leaders, even bosses you have worked for, pushed themselves just as hard?

Most of these people, whether you know them personally or have read about them, are even more critical of themselves. They push boundaries and give little or no excuses to 'be-ing'. Hence, accepting yourself with compassion is a great service, which will cause empathy to emanate from you. When you know and accept yourself, it becomes easy to deploy your gifts, talents and nuances, as you embark on this journey to success. Remember, the person you are today is a sum of all your experiences – good and bad, upbringing and environment – nothing should be hidden away!

Authenticity makes the process easier to bear: When you are in your elements, you thrive! And when you are thriving, you are productive! One of the signs that a person may not be living authentically is that they do not enjoy their job. It is important to note that, we have jobs where we earn a living, but we also have a mission – our impact, which is why we are here on earth.

A friend of mine shared the story of how she quit her job in the corporate world. She thought if she found a job with fewer hours she would be happy. She did find a job with fewer hours and she was really delighted at first; it seemed like that was what she was meant to be doing, but being the driven person that she is, she began to be noticed and with that came promotions and more money. You know the saying, 'The reward for hard work is more work!' She soon found herself in a bind and the cycle of discontent and misery resurfaced.

Soon enough, she realized that the reason she was so miserable was because she had not discovered what she was meant to be doing – her mission, that is, her aim and life's purpose. According to her, had she seen the bigger picture, it would have been easier to put up with her job a bit longer, and she would have had a more positive attitude, knowing it was just a means to an end. Instead, she saw her life as being just that, working at a stressful job, paying bills, looking after the home and that was it!

Her frustration came from her believing that life was not more than managing her job and her family. And she could not imagine spending the rest of her life doing that. But as she started to do a bit more introspection, she began to learn new skills and sharpen old ones; she employed the expertise of coaches, who helped her see further and clearly what her purpose was. Through this, she recognized what she would have done differently while remaining at her old (corporate) job and applying her engagements to prepare for her true mission.

When you are authentic, the process becomes easier because you will be operating within your natural strengths. Also, you will take criticisms more constructively and not beat yourself up too much for your failures. When you don't have to carry the baggage of trying to get people's validation, the journey becomes easier – you may feel hurt when people let you down or criticise you harshly, but you know better than stew over it and you know it is wise to move on to the many assignments lined up for you.

Authenticity extracts your creative juices: When you know what your strengths are, you can focus on them. There is something about focusing on what we do best because what we feed grows; you will begin to unravel different ways of achieving the same tasks. When you embrace your uniqueness, you become free enough to share your gift(s) with the world, and without fear. You begin to seek new ways to reach your audience, you begin to pay attention to the people that you have been assigned to share your gift(s) with – remember, you cannot save the world, nor have you been sent to everyone.

However, once you identify your target, you begin to find different ways to meet the unique needs of the individuals within your audience. People who are doing what they truly love often do it before they realize they could charge for their services. Money is hardly ever a factor in the work they do. Their minds are constantly at work seeking new ways to be a blessing. It is very difficult to achieve this if you are a copycat or if you are yet to find your unique purpose.

Authenticity makes people trust you: When you are authentic, people know they can trust you. Trust is highly underrated in today's world. There are business transactions that are sometimes conducted based on trust. Trust is such an invaluable trait, and it is something that authentic people possess. You earn people's trust when they discover that you are consistent and that your words and actions match.

Hindrances To Authenticity

If being authentic has so much value, why then do many people hide? Like I mentioned earlier, the view we have of ourselves and the world most times comes from our early exposure and upbringing. Many of us struggle with being our authentic selves because of:

Early life experiences: Growing up, I was a bubbly, happy and quite outspoken child but my parents got separated. I didn't realise at the time how it affected me, but I found out that I became someone who started to crave attention from other sources. I gave people more leeway than I gave myself. At this point, I was caught up in a damning perception of myself – I only mattered if people felt I mattered!

Thankfully, God opened my eyes to see and know differently. I started to learn that I was special, as I realised that some of the people from whom I sought validation were people who had not walked in my shoes, who did not know where I was headed and who in some cases, were headed nowhere themselves. I gave permission to be defined by the wrong people.

On the other hand, as I became more accepting of my unique self, I was able to see clearly how I was holding myself back by making other people more important in defining my life. I have to add that this self-discovery is not unconnected to my faith. It was when I came to faith that I started to get wind of how unique I was, and I learnt the truth of how 'I am fearfully and wonderfully made.' Now, I accept the fact that I can be me, even if it bothers people that I am a bubbly person; I don't have to be sad because the world is sad. I have embraced my authenticity and now I teach others to do the same. I am unapologetically me and I am living it out loud!

Lack of self-awareness: Again, as earlier mentioned, you cannot be authentic if you do not know yourself. You might need to do a personal assessment (many of those assessments are quite effective). You must be open to feedback, especially from people you know who have your best interest at heart. A friend of mine shared a story narrating how for several years, people saw her as rigid and too serious. Deep in her heart, she knew that was not who people thought she was; yet, she did not realize the extent to which she had built a wall around her. She often wondered why people tiptoed around her. In her own thoughts, she believed she was this very nice and kind person, which she truly was, but inadvertently kept hidden for fear of being taken for granted.

Fast forward to today, she tells me, she realizes she wants to be perceived as kind and generous. She has also learned to set boundaries and use her 'No' judiciously, so as not to be taken for granted. Mind you, her friendliness and empathy are key elements to her work as a therapist. Yet she has to manage her professional life and personal relationships, to avoid a clash or underplay, as the need arises.

Fear of exclusion: When we rely heavily on being accepted, it becomes quite hard to be ourselves. This reliance is also rooted in upbringing or early life experiences, where perhaps, if you were raised as a precocious child, you easily got into trouble or were isolated, to prevent others from your premature influence. The impact of such an experience could remain a painful memory in adulthood. You carry an emotional band-aid that can't be ripped nor forgotten, and this makes you constantly want to be with the crowd, looking for validation and never wanting to be excluded from the group. Growing up in poverty can also make you lose your authenticity, in the sense that you may pursue money for the confidence it gives you as a way of gaining acceptance from others. You may have a lot of money but may still feel insecure.

Have you encountered people who you know are way more financially endowed than you are and have more influence in society but still try to rub in the fact that they have more money than you? It comes from a place of insecurity and a need to be 'seen'.

How To Be Authentic

Know yourself: Seek self-awareness. This is the basis for authenticity.

Accept yourself: The good and the bad. Our bad experiences, flaws, as well as our good parts make up our unique personality – nothing is a mistake.

Don't hide yourself: While you maintain decorum and respect people's sensibilities, remember not to be bound by their expectations. You are worth being seen, you are endowed with solutions to meet people's needs, live your truth!

Align your decisions with your values: Let your values and beliefs reflect in your way of life and in the decisions you make.

Accept criticism: Remain open to feedback and do not be offended by it, even when you think it is in a bad taste. People often express themselves in ways that reflect who they are more than who you are.

Speak your mind, but with kindness: When you are upset, do not pretend that it doesn't matter. With you, let what people see and get be the same.

The place of being yourself in reaching your life's goals cannot be overemphasized. Without originality, you may make the money, but not make the impact; you are also less likely to impact a lot of people. Some people may only be able to relate with you because your uniqueness resonates with theirs, your experiences mirror theirs but if you hide that away, you will not be able to share your gift with them.

> *"If you are your authentic self, you have no competition."*
> *– Anonymous*

Think it out loud

Take a moment to reflect deeply, close your eyes if you like, and ask yourself these;

1. Who am I?
Note: Do not make any reference to your work or anything you do. Do not answer with reference to what you have. Who are you within your purpose?

2. What am I meant to be doing?
Once you identify who you are, your life's purpose becomes clearer.

A FRIEND CALLED PROCESS

CHAPTER THREE

Gaining New Knowledge.

*"Books are the quietest and most constant of friends;
they are the most accessible and wisest of counselors, and
the most patient of teachers"
- Charles. W. Eliot*

One habit that successful people share is their love for new knowledge. They read a lot!

Elon Musk is one of the most inspirational entrepreneurs of our time. His name is synonymous with Tesla and SpaceX. He is said to have read about 10 hours a day when he was in grade school. According to Elon, he gets his ideas from reading books. This same habit of reading is what has made others like Warren Buffett, Bill Gates, Mark Cuban, Oprah Winfrey, Jack Canfield, Anthony Robbins, Richard Branson, Mark Zuckerberg successful. (Source 1) In fact, if we do not seek information to gain new knowledge, we will not be successful.

People are very quick to point to the fact that Steve Jobs and Bill Gates dropped out of school. Truly, they did but that did not stop them from seeking information and gaining new knowledge. Having formal education does not necessarily equate to being successful. In some countries, people are more focused on the certificate than the actual knowledge acquired, which sometimes leads to people using unscrupulous means to get an education that they cannot defend, use to solve any real-life problems or even to improve themselves. Dropping out of formal school does not mean a person lacks education. If truth be told, formal schooling sometimes stifles our creativity. You may have little formal training but if you have an open mind and you are constantly learning, you will be successful.

There is very little progress we can make without gaining new mastery and improving our knowledge. The world has progressed from people hunting to feed their families, to discovery of fire; and from using stones to fashion weapons, to using irons. We have also moved from an agrarian society to industrialization; from the renaissance to today, we are in the information age. Every single progression the world has seen had modern knowledge underpinning it. What I am trying to point out is that, to make real progress, we must learn new skills.

Many times, people seek a job and they are so focused on earning their pay that it takes being relegated to the background, hiring or promoting a newer staff with more qualifications, or even being downsized for them to wake up to the reality that they need continuous learning to stay alive and afloat.

Sometimes, people ignore information about healthy lifestyle until they find themselves at the doctor's office dealing with an ailment that, could have been avoided by simply seeking and adhering to information. Sometimes, people destroy promising relationships because they refuse to seek knowledge that will help them navigate the complexities of their relationships. One of the most beneficial actions you can take in life is to seek recent knowledge and sharpen your skills. The world is changing at such a dynamic pace that if we do not move with it, we will find that our capacities may no longer serve us.

The ability to seek and utilize knowledge is one of the pillars my organization rests and thrives on. In the last thirteen years, I have consistently leveraged every opportunity to gain fresh knowledge and applied the same to my business. Upon realizing the constant pressure and demands placed on businesses, the emergence of technologies and the significance of social media, I knew that for me to achieve the type of relevance and growth I desire for my business, I must embrace the usage of social media, not just for personal and entertainment purposes like everyone can (post pictures, like, share or save a content). No! I needed to leverage the power of social media to grow my business. Hence, I enrolled in social media workshops and masterclasses, bought books and sought expert's opinion to move my business to the height it has attained.

Another thing I did, and still do is that I actively invest resources and time in books – leadership, business, and personal development. Not only do I engage in reading, but every member of my team is encouraged to do the same. Thus, we have been able to build a lasting learning culture that everyone now embraces. The importance cannot be overemphasized.

I understand my competencies, skills and need areas; I understand different leadership techniques, the best to adopt in different situations, and have a better working relationship with my team and clients. As a business, we are equipped with the skills and mental tools to achieve our goals, make better business decisions and easily navigate difficult situations because we are sold out to acquiring new knowledge.

In Japanese, the word 'Kaizen' is often associated with constant and continuous improvement and it is the principle behind how the Japanese handle everything in their lives – if you study the Japanese, you will see that all they do is synonymous with excellence and they are quickly improving and staying ahead. If we want to get ahead in life, to find our life's purpose, to know who we are and how to share our gifts with the world and be enriched by it, we need to continually be in pursuit of know-hows.

Gaining new knowledge could be getting further education in a formal setting, finding a coach, reading books, getting trained and becoming certified in a different field of study. You could check out a website that is relevant to the information you seek, make research on the internet, read journals and articles. You could also gain information by observing your environment or even mistakes as well as asking questions that will lead you to doing it correctly. If we are sensitive and alert, we will see all the information around us.

Why Seek New Knowledge?

You enhance your creativity and skill: When you seek new knowledge whether by reading a book, listening to a podcast, watching a video, further studies in a formal setting and so on, you are enhancing your knowledge. What this means is, you are not limited to what you know, you are gaining insight into what other people know – the mistakes they made and how they picked themselves up. You also become more knowledgeable about the bold steps they took and how you can also take such steps and avoid the pitfalls. You could save yourself years of heartbreak and frustration by hiring a coach to provide clarity in the direction you are seeking to take. Alternatively, help could come through a book. Seeking information opens our mind and enhances our creativity; we not only begin to learn new ways of doing things but even new ways of thinking, which in my opinion is the most important benefit of gaining new knowledge.

Personal development: Seeking new mastery helps you become a different person. In chapter one, I mentioned that sometimes people ask us to 'be ourselves'; and while that is good advice, most times, we need an improved version of ourselves to meet our life goals. If my work requires me to be more jovial but I am naturally shy, being myself will hinder me greatly. I may need to become a friendlier person even if it is just to enable me get the tasks done. So, getting help, like coaching and new tools, such as networking, to become more confident will help you thrive as an individual. Reading on how to build your confidence will be of great benefit to you because seeking information not only shows us what to do but likewise, how we must be.

Motivation: If you are feeling down and out and you feel at your wits end, reading or watching inspiring stories about successful people can motivate and transport you to a world of new possibilities. With an open mind you become energized and you can see beyond your current circumstances because there is an inlet of many transformational ideas. You will also acquire new tools to help you solve your problems as well as learn the process of critical thinking and creativity – skills required to excel in life.

One of the most impactful books I have read is *Everyone communicates but not everyone connects* by John C Maxwell, it helped me see my abilities beyond being a speaker. It taught me that I can only make an impact in the lives of people connected to me. I have also benefited tremendously from Fela Durotoye's podcast. Learning is a gift that can give us a mindset shift. There isn't a successful person, who has not been motivated by some information, they learned about someone they admired.

Develop confidence: Self-expression is an art that stems from acquiring new skills or seeking new information. It is no secret that reading greatly improves one's vocabulary, which in turn, helps improve the art of communication, which then boosts confidence. Being exposed to several areas of life, offers a clearer and more explorative picture of life. This not only shows your abilities, it also places you in a high value space, and this is a confidence booster.

Versatility and Adaptability: The future of work is changing; hence, it is imperative to have an open and adaptable mindset. According to a report by the World Economic Forum, Future of Jobs Report (2020), half of all workers will need to re-skill by 2025. (Source 2) That means we need to learn new skills to be able to fit into the world that will be at that time. A teachable person is already equipped for the future because the future is for learners – learners have a growth mindset. Learning skills helps you become adaptable and versatile. You may suffer a job loss, but you are able to bounce back because you are open to learning. This is such a valuable skill to acquire in today's world.

In recent times, the most sought-after skills have less to do with the core literacies and more to do with social and emotional learning and intelligence. What use is a brilliant scientist who has difficulty managing his emotions? What use is a brilliant entrepreneur who becomes frustrated at obstacles rather than seeking to solve the problems that arise. Critical thinking and problem-solving are the top skills that employers believe will grow in prominence in the next five years. Post-pandemic skills that are emerging and relevant are self-management, active learning, resilience, stress tolerance and flexibility. All of which can be learned by being receptive to new information.

Leverage: Information is so important that it can unbutton you up to a whole new world of opportunities. Having relevant information is the difference between being aware of an investment opportunity that will change your life and being broke. Having relevant information is the difference between making a sound decision in your relationships and being damaged by bad relationships. With information, you have an advantage over those walking blind.

> *"The beautiful thing about learning is that*
> *no one can take it from you."*
> *- B.B.King*

How to seek information

Identify your learning need: Have you recently lost your job and want to know how to get past that? A simple google search on what to do after losing your job would be of great assistance. You could talk to a friend about your job loss too. Do you need to improve your relationship? You could buy a book that addresses the relationship goals you are trying to achieve. Identify the need you have, then seek the relevant information to help you.

Identifying the most effective approach: Do you need to upskill? Are you pursuing a place in academia and need to go for further learning? Do you need to hire a business coach or a relationship coach? Will you be okay just reading a book and snippets from social media or articles from a blog? The level of upskilling you need and the extent of the impact you want to make will determine the most effective approach you should seek.

Apply the knowledge gained: Doing this will help you see how feasible what you are learning is and how you can adapt it to your peculiar situation. You will know whether to seek more knowledge in that area or learn a complementary skill.

Surround yourself with people who have the same goals: Are you a coach? Seek out other coaches to help sharpen each other. Do you seek to improve your relationships? Seek people who have such objectives; they could be people you can interact with physically or within a virtual community, to exchange ideas and sharpen each other.

Be curious about other fields: Don't be narrow in your search for information. Read widely, learn new skills. Everything in life is interdependent and interwoven, so it helps to be knowledgeable about a number of topics. Being informed in a language even if it is just a few words might be the key to opening a door you have been knocking at for a long time. Being knowledgeable about a topic you might consider irrelevant to your work, might be what you need to break into a particular industry or organization you have been working hard to enter. While it is not necessary to be an expert in every field, it is important to have a few ideas about a lot of topics.

Don't overdo it: Seek knowledge for the value it brings to you and others, not as a measure of your worth or as a tool to bring others down. There are people who feel compelled to be in the know about everything, they take over conversations at every opportunity and never allow people to contribute. Their self-worth is tied to their ability to have an opinion about every subject. They find it difficult to admit to not knowing. They want to be seen as the go-to person for information. While being like that is a good thing in the sense that you may have answers to a lot of questions, if seeking information is simply so you can feel worthy, you may not have enough depth to use all your information as a tool to solve real problems. You may be able to say what you have read but may not be able to use that information in practical terms to solve a problem. In that instance, information is more of a burden than a blessing.

Think it out loud

What book or books have you read in the last 6 months?

In what ways have they impacted you?

Task

Within the next one month, find a book to read in an area of life that you need mentoring or improvement. Note how the book impacts you.

References

Source 1
(https://www.thewisdompost.com/reading/billionaires-and-their-reading-habits/1073)

Source 2
(https://www.weforum.org/agenda/2020/10/top-10-work-skills-of-tomorrow-how-long-it-takes-to-learn-them/)

Source 3
(https://www.weforum.org/reports/the-future-of-jobs-report-2020/in-full/infographics-e4e69e4de7)

A FRIEND CALLED PROCESS

CHAPTER FOUR

Mastering Your Craft

"We are what we repeatedly do. Excellence,
then, is not an act, but a habit."
— Aristotle

D you know what differentiates an expert or someone who mentors others from everyone else? Have you wondered how some people come to become experts in their field? It's beyond sheer interest and innate abilities; these people have honed their skills over time and have mastered their craft. In the previous chapter, we discussed acquiring new knowledge, which we established is a critical foundation for a successful life. In this chapter, we will be looking at the next level – what do you do after gaining new knowledge? What do you do with the new information? How do you handle the newly acquired information by applying it to becoming exceptional or becoming a master in your field?

K. Anders Ericsson, in his 1993 paper, *The Role of Deliberate Practice in the Acquisition of Expert Performance*, posited that being exceptional in one's field reflects deliberate effort to improve performance in one's area of work. He added that the people we call geniuses did not arrive at their expertise because of innate talent but by putting in countless hours of work before earning the right to be called experts. Mastery therefore, is a destination that is achievable by anyone, as long as they are willing to put in the work to achieve it.

What then, is mastery? *Mastery is a special state of mind in which the skill runs almost entirely within the unconscious (Johannsen, 1986).* Mastery is becoming an expert in a skill. It is having the ability to teach something and being the best at what you do. Achieving mastery as earlier mentioned takes a lot of work. The first rule of mastery is practice over and over again!

A good example of people who have achieved mastery in their work are athletes. If you consider tournaments like the Olympics, to win a gold medal at any of these events requires hours of unrelenting practice and preparedness. Mastery requires you to continue even when you feel like giving up. It obliges you to make immense sacrifices and self-denials. It demands that you keep your eyes on the goal. When you think of masters at their craft, names like Serena and Venus Williams come to mind, others will be Michelangelo, Mohammed Ali, Pele, Mozart, Michael Jackson, Michael Phelps. All these people became synonymous with their craft: Michael Jackson for instance was and still is known as the

King of Pop. The name, Michael Phelps immediately brings swimming to mind; and of course, the Williams sisters bring tennis to mind. It's a no-brainer that Michelangelo is foremost on the mind for painting or art. That is mastery!

You see, mastery births recognition; what this means is it brings you to a position whereby whenever people think of a niche or a specific area of need, your name or business pops up as an expert to provide the solution they desire. My charity organisation; The Esther's Company attained this status when it got nominated for the Queen's Award for Voluntary Service in 2021. The feeling was surreal! Even though, we did not win the award, it felt great to know that the work we do by providing support for the black community in Glasgow, was recognized and thought worthy of an award. This could only be achieved because we have consistently stayed true to our goals, even when it didn't make sense and the journey seemed bleak, we stayed true till we mastered our craft.

Have you ever heard the saying, 'When you do something you love, you would never have to work again in your life'. In a sense, mastery gets easier with identifying reason. Mastering a skill especially in an area that aligns with your core values gives you a sense of direction and purpose. It makes practice easier than if you are trying to master something you are not particularly suited for. As time goes on, your mind is able to adapt to the process, and you become more consistent, disciplined and focused on your goals. This focus gives you the push and momentum you need to keep going.

In the same light, we are going to analyse the phrase, *Jack of all trades, master of none* – a very popular phrase. Sometimes, people want to do so many things at the same time, while versatility is a great skill to possess, multi-tasking does not allow absolute focus to make the right kind of impact you are capable of. I have a friend who each time we chat, will tell me about one new business that she is doing.

She is so excited about her many businesses and she is more focused about making money than becoming an expert. In her case, that might work for her but is she making an impact? If attaining all round success is your goal, you have to drill down to an area that you can focus on. Sometimes it is difficult for people who are multi-talented to show bias to one skill. They feel like they are missing out on something because there are so many things they do well. However, in the case of a person whose goal is to make an impact, there is a driver, and something keeps them up at night. Questions that beg for answers, solutions to more growth and impact… and the list is endless.

Ponder on this: What would you do as you are doing now even if you didn't make any money from it? The answers from this thought will help narrow your focus. To become a master, you have to narrow down.

Why Gain Mastery in Your Skill?

"The happiness of a man in this life does not consist in the absence but in the mastery of his passions." – Alfred Lord Tennyson.

You Become Your Authentic Self: With honing our skills, two things happen; we begin to realize what is really important to us and put in the work required to bring our craft to life – with this, the sacrifice gets easier.

At the start of this chapter, I mentioned a list of people who have become masters in their craft, and whose names have become synonymous with their craft. This is as a result of mastering their craft. When you seek mastery, you begin to adapt to who you are deep down and you are able to share that gift with the world.

Life Satisfaction: When our life purpose is not known, when we are simply coasting along, we are likely to have a sense of unfulfillment and a lack of satisfaction in life. Discovering your gift and putting in the time and effort to master it, gives you a sense of purpose, a perception that you are contributing to life. That feeling that you have written and published a book or that you have completed a project, there is nothing compared to the rewards that come from sharing your gifts. It is important to mention that, you do not have to be a perfect craftsman, you do not have to write a bestseller but you do need to be striving to be better than you were, the last time. As you strive, the world will notice, you will make an impact, receive accolades and find fulfilment.

Growth: In seeking mastery, we are compelled to grow. Constantly pursuing and improving our craft will continue to open doors. You may be invited to speak and you will meet people who will enhance your life. Several job opportunities may even be in the offing. You will get more recognition, especially because your work now speaks for you in places and rooms you can't be in. *Achieving mastery requires you to come out of your comfort zone and become more fearless.* Therein lies your growth; you become a better version of yourself and start on a path that you may never have envisioned.

As tasking as mastery gets, its rewards are immeasurable. The sense of fulfilment isn't something you would want to trade for anything else. Mastery is worth it!

Financial Reward: As a coach, I know that some of the most expensive coaches are also some of the most experienced. They are experienced because of the time it has taken to garner the experience, and even, what it has cost them to be trained for such delicate roles, handling people's careers and futures in their hands. This is why they invest thousands of hours mastering their craft.

If as a coach, you pay $600 for a course, you will not be afraid to charge $600 for your own course. The greater the price you pay for mastery, the more you can demand and expect from your clients. The more you have mastered your craft, the more aware you are of its peculiarities and the more you will be able to help people. This usually translates to more financial rewards.

Barriers to Mastering Your Craft

Not seeing the bigger picture: Without the bigger picture, the focus will be blurry and on the immediate objective or short-term goals, like what pays in the short term, or in the now. Many times, when we hear people's success stories, we assume everything happened within a short time and so when we start our own journey and it doesn't happen, then we throw in the towel. Another story of a friend who shared her experience about journeying the entrepreneurial route. She had quit her job because she wanted to work at her own pace and leave the rat race. At that time, the rat race was affecting her family life and even her health. Her expectation was that within six months, her business would begin to flourish.

You are probably laughing reading this, if you have managed to build a successful business. She believed all she needed was to believe in what she was doing. Well, it did not turn out that way and she eventually had to go back to get a job. If she had dedicated more time to finding further information and honing her skills, she may have realised soon enough that it took longer than 6 months and a stretch of consistency.

Perhaps, after two years, she might have started to glimpse what life as a business owner would look like. Her desire to work at her own pace might have started to materialize if only she could see the bigger picture. She was immediately overwhelmed with the teething phase every entrepreneur encounters, and soon after, she gave up. Whatever your goals are, whatever outcome you want to achieve, you must be intentional about it. You can only be intentional if you know what you are working towards – you must focus on the bigger picture!

Reluctance to pay the price: Sometimes when people catch a glimpse of the sacrifice it would take to attain their goals, they give up. Do you want to be a master in your field? Or is your goal to lose weight? Are you aiming to become a better parent or to build a successful business? Every one of these goals require some level of sacrifice. *Of course, the more mastery you desire, the more the sacrifice* – there is the constant search and upgrade of your knowledge. You may even need to go back to acquire a new formal degree, or spend a lot of money to become a certified practitioner in your field.

For those pursuing a weight loss goal, there are certain lifestyles and diets you may need to adopt to be in better shape or health. And if you are on the path to emotional recovery, you may need to set boundaries with certain friends and family for as long as you need to heal. Oftentimes, people do not want to pay the price; perhaps because of the fear of negative feedback, or being ridiculed. This stunts our growth and keeps us from achieving mastery. We settle for playing on the side-lines because that is where everybody is – and it is a comfort zone. Getting ahead requires doing more and sometimes, we are not even ready for the new or next level.

Focusing on immediate gratification: There is also the possibility that when people set out to pursue their life goals, they are dealing with some financial difficulty. The focus then shifts from impact to pursuance of wealth – how to make money from the work they are doing. In situations as such, there is a reluctance to spend money on self-development to bring them closer to mastery in their chosen field. The money may then be diversified to meet other pressing financial needs. It takes a tremendous amount of discipline to invest in personal or professional development, especially when you have other pressing domestic responsibilities – a family and bills to settle. This is the true test of sacrifice. In this instance, the person will struggle to achieve mastery and may find it difficult to progress beyond where they are.

How to Become a Master in Your Field

When people are hailed for their excellence, we do not see the hours of toiling, tears and sometimes, shame that went into that foundation. All we get to see is their spectacular performances, or hear about the money they make, which we easily desire for ourselves. We hear of the impact they are making in a particular field and we want to be like them. However, we must be ready to put in the hours, maybe years or even a lifetime of learning, refining and sharing our gift(s). If you want to become a master in your field, below are a few steps, you can take to arrive at greatness:-

Get a job: Strange? When you work, you will find your purpose. When I relocated to the UK eighteen years ago, it was not out of desperation. Yes, I sought greener pastures, but the pastures back home in Nigeria were green enough. I had a good job and I was doing relatively well, but I knew there was more to life and I was certain that if I stayed back in Nigeria, I would not be afforded the opportunity to make the level of impact that I wanted.

Meanwhile, once in the United Kingdom, my passion for starting a charity and impacting lives began to burn, even in the midst of the rat race I had become entangled. Still, I knew I now had the enabling environment I always sought to pursue that dream. The environment was more supportive of goals such as mine, and like I mentioned, my charity was nominated for the Queen's Award for Voluntary Services 2021. It takes a level of mastery for your work to be recognized for the highest award for the voluntary sector in the United Kingdom. How is this connected to getting a job? You might ask. When you work, you will find your purpose; either because your job fires you up, gives you fulfilment or otherwise.

If you find out that you are unhappy at work, you may start to seek answers about your purpose. When you find your purpose, passion will most likely propel you to seeking mastery. So, it all starts with becoming engaged. Always find something for your hands to do, or better yet, start with what is available to you.

Focus on learning: Focus on your growth; and once you identify your goal, focus on learning. At this point, you may want to volunteer at an organisation that caters for your passion, so you can gain the skills you need to grow. You might want to seek out a mentor, so you can learn first-hand how they have built their businesses or practices. The easiest way to seek out a mentor is to follow them closely. For those too far to reach, you may follow their works closely and if they have features or published works – journals, articles or books, get into their heads by reading their publications, listening to their podcasts or interviews, paying and attending their courses.

With growth comes distractions; it is just as easy to plan to be focused as it is to be easily distracted. Staying mindful and acknowledging there are stumbling blocks may help. Identify the distractions and plan to nip them in the bud. It is futile and fatal to ignore them, or assume they do not matter. If you begin to look around you and see what others are doing, or you find out that social media readily presents you updates on people you think you are better than who seem to be doing much better than you, this can lead a person to insecurity, causing you to focus on perception – being seen, rather than working hard behind the scenes, and delivering results.

Share your knowledge: Look for opportunities to share your knowledge. Use your social media platforms, organize virtual seminars, ask people to speak at your event for free. This will help you build a followership that you can leverage on later. A lot of people will not understand what you are doing but you are not on a show, you are building a life – your future – so you must focus on that. Accept as many options as possible to share your knowledge. Don't let the fact that you are not yet 'an expert' make you hide away. Don't worry about what others are doing, just focus on your own growth. Remember to constantly add value to those who are following and listening to you, no matter how small the number.

Stretch yourself: Move out of your comfort zone! We all know this but somehow it is so hard to do. If you continue to do things the same way repeatedly, you will hit a plateau, which means you stop growing. Gaining mastery in your craft requires you to do things that may be uncomfortable most of the time. A lot of people dread speaking in front of others, but it may be a requirement for you on your way to achieving your goals. To master a skill, think of something you need to do but also find uncomfortable, then do it. It could be recording and sharing a video of yourself or speaking to a small audience at first; it could be talking about what you do and why you do it or learning to sell your idea to an ideal client, it could be putting your ideas into a book or accepting to speak at an event… whatever it is, remember comfort is an enemy of success.

So, break the mould and worry less about 'what ifs' – So what if you make a mistake? What if you don't sound perfect? You will make mistakes! Everyone does. People will criticize you! It comes with the territory, but you will not know growth if you do not permit yourself to stretch. Also, to experience exponential growth, you need to stretch beyond your personal boundaries. With this, you will become a much better version of yourself; one who is more confident and competent. The question is, are you willing to pay the price?

Be willing to fail: One of the biggest reasons people fear to take a step towards mastery is the fear of failure. They fear they may not succeed; however, this new age is teaching us that the opposite of success is ideally not failure, it is "not trying" – you are only a failure when you do not try. What I have found over the years to be at the core of people who fear is not really the fact that they may fail, it is more about how they will be viewed by people if they fail. However, we hardly get motivated by what if you succeed – and this is good enough to make an attempt. *So, the fear of failure for many is really the fear of what people would say.*

Criticism is indeed a hard pill to swallow, especially when you are out there, working on your growth. So many people want to play safe and end up staying small. Meanwhile, to become a master at your craft, you will need to aim high and sometimes, in aiming high, you may fall, but never lose sight of your goal. It is a part of the 'learning and becoming' process and it never really ends. The challenges change as you grow but failing is a part of growth and it is vital for succeeding at our life's goal. What happens over time is that you are better able to manage your emotions when you fail and you make fewer careless mistakes. Failure is important because it develops your ability to think more creatively and deeper, birthing creative solutions that you may not have thought of if you had not failed. The extent to which we are willing to embrace failure as a part of the process will determine the extent to which we succeed.

Remember this, mastery does not insist on you being perfect, it only requires that you show up consistently, be bold and unrelenting. It requires you to put your heart and soul into your work and believe me, it will be worth it in the end.

"To become a master at any skill, it takes the total effort of your: heart, mind, and soul working together in tandem."
- Maurice Young

Think it out loud

- On a scale of 1 to 10, how would you rate your level of mastery in your craft?

- What are you doing to become an expert in your field?

A FRIEND CALLED PROCESS

CHAPTER FIVE

Consistency

"I have lost almost 300 games, 26 times. I have been trusted to take the game winning shot and missed. I have failed over and over and over again in my life and that is why I succeed."

This statement above has been credited to
Michael Jordan.

Can you dare to fail 300 times? Can you dare to show yourself some empathy if you miss the winning shot? Can you dare to fail over and over and over again? That is what it takes to be a winner. That is what it takes to succeed. That is what consistency is – showing up as your best self, regardless. Many of us are so afraid of failing that the moment we see that we may miss the winning shot, we move on to something else. Some of us have started four, five, six businesses within ten years with nothing to show for it. Like the friend I mentioned earlier, we tend to think that once we set out to achieve our goals, everything will happen within six months. At the heart of mastering our craft is consistency!

To be consistent means you are doing the same things over and over, in a bid to reach your goal. To be consistent means you are showing up when you must. If for instance, you have a goal of bagging an academic Master's, to be consistent will mean, to attend your classes, to do your tasks, to show up for the exams and to write your thesis. If you fail to show up consistently, you will not get your Master's degree. If you have a goal to lose weight and you have a plan to walk two miles every day, if you show up once a week sometimes and don't show up at all another week and show up twice a week another time, you will not reach your expectation. So, it is with our life goals.

Being consistent is not a walk in the park. In fact, at some point you might get discouraged and frustrated, especially when people consider your ideas superfluous, unattainable or overly ambitious, or when the results are not forthcoming despite the effort you exert. I recall my early years in business, I met people who I thought would key into my ideas and grow my business with me. After letting them in on my ideas and visions, some of them outrightly backed out as my ideas seemed 'too big', while some others who journeyed with me soon began getting discouraged, seeing that it was not yielding as quickly as they expected and they were unsure if it ever would, so they eventually pulled out too. But you see, I persisted and constantly chased my dreams. Truth is, as a business owner, you own the vision, so more than anybody else, you understand your purpose for pursuing that venture and its importance to you. For me, it was more about making an impact and fulfilling my purpose than maximizing profit.

What are you aiming to achieve? Have you been talking about starting your own business? What small steps are you taking towards that goal? In what ways are you showing up towards your vision? Being consistent is to stick to your principles, to be steadfast and to show up with the same dispositions about where you are headed. You are confident about your aspirations and you pursue them without distraction. When you are consistent, your eyes are on the target; you may change your strategy, you may go back to the drawing board but your eyes are always on the goal and you are working towards them.

Why Should You Be Consistent?

How do you feel when you know someone always keeps to their word? You develop trust, right? That is what consistency does. When you show up in your space, people begin to trust what you have to say, and they begin to understand that you will be there when they come knocking. In Nigeria, a lot of people have small, neighbourhood (mom & pop) shops where they sell groceries and beverages. Many of these shops are scattered around most residential areas. One thing these shop owners have learned, is to tell customers, '*Oh, I will go to the market tomorrow to restock, I don't have it now*'. They say this whether they intend to restock or not. To them, it keeps the clients coming back and they feel it is safer to say, '*I will have what you need tomorrow*', than to say, '*We don't sell that item*'. Not a good way to go about consistency but they understand that people want to be able to get what they want when they want it or you will lose them.

I will be looking at five reasons why it is important to be consistent as you grow in your craft and desire to succeed in it.

You become disciplined: Many of us struggle with habits that require discipline, and in my opinion, I believe this is the hardest value to build as you develop yourself. When you are consistent, you learn new habits which are in line with the outcome you want to see. Often, you do not get rewarded immediately and consistency expects that you keep at it, regardless. This behaviour develops discipline and self-control. Take for instance, you want to lose weight and you have a plan to work out three times a week and keep certain foods out of your diet.

Consistency means saying no to the temptation to go back to eating those foods that may not be good for you. Consistency means getting up and doing that work-out even when you do not feel like it, or even when you do not yet see the results. After a while, you would habitually fall into routine with the activities – eating healthy foods, exercising often, and if you miss it for a day, your body knows. Developing self-control and self-discipline is one of the most important reasons for being consistent.

People trust you: When you are consistent, you demonstrate that you can lead yourself, you can trust yourself to show up when you need to. Being consistent means that you are taking control of your circumstances. This makes people to also trust you. There are certain people who would ask you for a loan, and you would lend them without questions because over time, they have demonstrated a sense of commitment to paying back what they owe. They respect themselves and respect people enough to not take the goodwill of others for granted. There are certain employees that have gained the trust of their superiors that in a short time of being employed, they are given responsibilities that people who have stayed longer were not offered. When you are consistent, people know what to expect from you thereby, causing you to earn their trust.

You have good progress: When you are consistent, you will find that you are accomplishing your goals faster than you envisaged. You will also be better prepared for opportunities that come your way than if you were inconsistent. What people call an overnight success, is simply someone working consistently, and then having an opportunity. Robert Kiyosaki in his book, **'Before you quit your job'** shared a story about how he and his team had created the CASHFLOW game to teach people how to be financially literate. He had been working on that game; testing, refining, and then one day, he got invited to Oprah's show and it seemed as if he just came out of nowhere. He would not have been ready to be on that show had he not been consistently working on his dream.

You become accountable: One thing consistent people do is to create routines that make it hard to back out of, even if they wanted to. Dates validate our commitment – so, they may announce a seminar with dates on social media, which means you have committed to it. Now, it is out there, and you can't change your mind as you like. You may share your action plan with a trusted friend and permit them to follow up on you. This builds accountability into the person and helps them achieve the results they are looking for.

Why We Struggle With Being Consistent

> *"Small disciplines repeated with consistency every day lead to great achievements gained slowly over time."*
> *– John Maxwell*

Those small disciplines, repeated with consistency over time is why many people struggle with consistency. The hardest part of being consistent is to show up day in, day out and have *nothing* to show for it. They tell you, to open an account on Instagram, to post at least three times a week, to do live videos, to share testimonials, to do something fun, to do giveaways, to do challenges. You do it all and still, it seems you haven't made much headway. Many of us want to achieve results and achieve it now!

Below are some of the reasons why:

Inability to Wait: Many of us have a wrong idea of what it takes to be successful, and this is why we set out to build a business and expect that in 6 months to one year, we would have built a huge empire. We then become discouraged when we encounter obstacles, which we must. We begin to think time is against us and we can't keep doing this without results. A lot of people find it hard to wait for the outcomes of their hard work to yield, and they erroneously believe if they do not see immediate results, then it must not be worth it. Many people give up their dreams at this point. They may then move on to other things they believe will be easier to do and quicker to succeed in. Focusing on the outcomes we want, rather than the process, can make one quit the journey abruptly. As much as we want to have positive outcomes, if we are constantly watching and waiting for these only, we will be discouraged and tempted to quit the process of becoming successful.

Poor Sense of Clarity and Focus: One thing that is quite common that I have seen in this generation is people copying other people's ideas because it is working. You will hear people say, 'Mr X started the bottled water business and now he has *made it*; I think you should consider going into bottled water business '. Many people lack a sense of purpose. For them, the goal is to make money first, and most times all of the mission is to just make money. When your goal is simply to make money, if it doesn't happen in the shortest time possible, you would begin to lose concentration and begin to consider other options. Sometimes, people are also not so sure about their purpose, they do not have a strong conviction that they should be doing what they are doing especially if, they find no one else is doing it. They may feel discouraged and think perhaps nobody wants their services, not realizing that they could actually be trailblazers in that field. A sense of purpose and focus on their objectives will help them stay focused and consistent as they pursue their dreams.

Limiting Beliefs: The mind is a very powerful tool, but how well are we wielding it? If we think we may not be good at something, the moment we hit a brick wall, we begin to doubt ourselves and may consider pulling back. Someone with a more positive mindset will see the obstacle as a learning opportunity, make the necessary adjustments and continue on their journey. When I wanted to start The Esther's Company; my charity organization, I was really in doubt about how to proceed. I was worried about how people would receive it, and if they would approve it. I was concerned about how people would see me, and what they would say but I realized if I wanted to make any progress, I had to change my limiting beliefs and that was exactly what I did.

Poor Habits: With poor habits, we will struggle to be consistent because it demands a level of discipline, delayed gratification and accountability. Many of us are not naturally equipped with the skills we need to succeed in life.

The most successful people in the world are known to be avid readers and knowledge seekers. Those are definitely habits we must develop if we are to be successful, and it compels us to be consistent in doing it. If we fail to develop these habits, we will not get the positive outcomes we seek. If we have negative habits of maybe procrastinating or even refusing to be accountable, we will not achieve the goal we are aiming towards.

Lack of Self-Compassion: Align this with discipline as well. When we have the wrong views about consistency, when we believe that to be consistent means never ever failing, we become rigid in our thinking and this hampers our ability to show up. Some people believe if they fail at a task or they are unable to show up once, then they must be irresponsible. They do not spare themselves and punish themselves harshly for mistakes made. This can make the journey burdensome and impossible in some cases. We must understand that there is no such thing as 100% consistency. If we do not allow ourselves periods of grace, we will burn out and our work will amount to nothing.

How To Be Consistent

Becoming consistent doesn't need to be a chore. It is such an important habit that it is necessary to devise a means to ensure we are showing up as regularly as possible. Below are some of the ways we can show up without burning out:-

Take baby steps: It always helps to break down our tasks into smaller tasks and tackle one before moving to the other. Attempting to take on huge tasks all at once will lead to discouragement, fatigue and an awareness that you cannot achieve your goals. If you want to write a book for instance, decide what your topic will be. Identifying what resources you will need, where you will source your material, how much time you will spend per day, what will go into your chapter one, breaking it into such manageable tasks will make the process way easier than if you didn't have a clear picture in mind. A lack of clear focus on how you want to go about it will wear you out and you may end up never writing that book.

Have a to-do list: One thing I have found is to schedule all my activities on my calendar. This helps me measure my progress as well as, keep tabs on what needs to be done. One benefit of having a to-do list is the feeling of achievement you get when you tick a task off your list. The feeling that you are making progress fosters productivity and consistency. Creating a to-do list or a schedule helps you stay on track.

Make it fun: One of the ways teachers make learning fun for children is to sometimes come up with fun activities the students can do; sometimes, they role play, sing nursery rhymes, or mnemonics (which also helps with memory improvement). And sometimes, a reward system is used to encourage participation in the lesson. You can do the same for yourself to help you remain consistent. What fun thing can you associate being consistent with? Can you promise to focus on your task for one straight hour or for one day and then take a fun break? Maybe dance to your favourite song a little or go for a walk. Can you find a fun activity that you can do alongside your work? For some people listening to music helps as they strategize, others need to have some noise while brainstorming perhaps over lunch? What do you think will help you? Make your journey fun-filled!

Mind how you spend your time: It is important to take a break from work to avoid burning out. However, it is also very easy to idle away and waste time. What I recommend when you feel your mind drifting away is to take a short break and then come back to work refreshed. When you structure your work and play time that way, it gives you something to look forward to – to break monotony – also makes it easy to remain focused. Someone recommended that we focus on our work and resist the urge to check our phones for at least 30 minutes. What you will find is that if you are able to focus for 15 minutes without going to your phone, you are usually able to work for at least an hour straight. Obviously, being able to avoid distractions helps you cover more ground and keeps you moving forward .

Find an accountability partner: This is actually easier said than done; it isn't all the time that people are able to show up in a beneficial way to you. However, if you know you really struggle with being a self-starter or with being motivated, I will recommend you find someone who will be happy to provide that support to you. Some people are natural self-starters and know how to pace and motivate themselves; unfortunately, there are others who need a constant prodding until they get to a point of minimal push and, gradually make their way to being consistent performers. If you are someone who needs that push, ask for help. And here is the thing, when your accountability partner checks up on you, make sure you do not come up with excuses; one excuse begets another and you do not want to push them out. So, you have to make sure, it is worth their while helping you achieve your goals.

Just do it: Many times, we will struggle to do the things we really need to do; I have learnt that sometimes, all we need is to just do it. No need to over-analyze or overthink it; just do it! Often, we are held back by fear – the fear of failure or the fear of mockery from people – all kinds of distractions. But in *just doing it*, we break the hold that fear has on us and we are able to move things much further along. We must realize that people are often more afraid of the shame that comes from being criticized or ridiculed than from the actual failure. When we just do what it is we need to do, more often than not, our plans go better than we expect; our confidence grows, and we are able to keep up the pace. So, if you find yourself overthinking the next phase of your business or any idea at all, just do it. Take your time to gather helpful information, but know that you have to act eventually.

Here are a few questions to reflect on as you build your consistency.

- What is that one goal you want to achieve this month or year?
- What strategies have you identified to help you reach your goals?
- How consistent are you in taking action?
- What obstacles have you faced and surmounted?
- How did you surmount them?
- If you are still struggling, what do you think you can do differently to overcome those obstacles? Can you read a book to learn from someone else's perspective? Can you (afford to) change your strategy? Can you possibly seek some advice?

If we learn to be consistent, we will achieve our goals. On the other hand, if we are not consistent, our goals will not be accomplished.

"Success isn't always about greatness. It's about consistency. Consistent hard work leads to success. Greatness will come."
– Dwayne Johnson

Think it out loud

- In what ways do you personally struggle to be consistent?
- What can you begin to do right now to become more consistent?
- What evidence will you see to show you are making progress?
- Who will hold you accountable?

CHAPTER SIX

Opportunity

*"Opportunities are presented to us each and every day,
but do we see them? To see an opportunity, we must be
open to all thoughts."*
- Catherine Pulsifer

Growing up, I often heard people say '*Opportunity comes but once.*' I can't tell you the tremendous pressure that used to put me under. I believed that once I lost an opportunity, it was gone forever and I was stuck for life! Looking back, I find it all so funny but I understand the idea behind that statement to mean we must always be ready to seize opportunities as they present themselves to us. When I think of opportunities, I think of the openings you become aware of and which come to you as a result of taking consistent and purposeful actions in all you do.

An opportunity is a situation that helps you attain your goals. Usually, they are favourable to you but may not always appear as such – some manifest in form of a challenge and our reaction to it or the need to find a solution makes it an opportunity.

Opportunities abound, they are all around us. They will come to us if we are ready, we will see the opportunity in every situation that life presents us and turn them into gifts.

How to Attract Opportunities

Even though opportunities are all around us, they won't just fall on our laps. We have to recognize and take advantage of them. How then can we attract opportunities?

Be a risk taker: This is one of the hardest things for people to do. Stop worrying, it takes too much energy and time to worry; instead, put yourself out there and take the risk. Remember we have talked about the 'just do it' effect. To attract opportunities, you have to put yourself out there, be bold to take that new step, and perhaps, join that business club. Whatever you do, take a calculated risk, knowing in your guts, that it will eventually pay off. I have previously spoken about my struggle with limiting beliefs; wondering what people would say about what I wanted to pursue and being hesitant.

None of the successes I have achieved in my work would have happened if I had gone on to hide (myself) away. Most people you see and read about doing phenomenal works started out with similar fears; many still struggle with self-doubt even at the peak of their careers, but they know they must act and keep putting themselves out there. If you want your message to be heard, if you want your product to be bought; then you must put yourself out there. This could mean creating your own speaking opportunity or writing your own book; it could mean joining a financial literacy club, enrolling for a course, or meeting new people and learning new perspectives. You could follow value-adding influencers on social media, and comment on their posts; go even further by joining their community.

Endure discomfort: What could you do today, as a sacrifice so that you can put your feet up tomorrow, knowing they could yield? I know so many people who are passionate about their work, competent and full of value but too afraid of doing live videos on social media. Some are even afraid to open a social media account to share their thoughts, they imagine they would come across as unserious, or that friends will make fun of them. They worry that they will be criticized or judged for speaking their truth.

There will never be a time when people will not judge you. In fact, the more successful you are, the more likely the chance of being criticized harshly; so why delay the 'evil day'? To become successful in life, you must be willing to endure discomfort. A friend was sharing her experience as a secondary school teacher and she told me about two colleagues who found teaching a particular year group cumbersome. They didn't enjoy the syllabus for that group; they found it boring and a little difficult to teach and so when she joined the school, both her colleagues dumped the whole year group on her.

She found the topics boring as well but decided she was going to do something about it, and that she did. She found fun ways to teach those classes and managed to turn things around. She became sort of an expert in teaching the topics and her resourcefulness did not go unnoticed by the school management which led to promotions for her sooner than she or anyone expected. She became a go-to person in the department and became extremely valuable in the school. That was an opportunity that her colleagues gave up because they were not willing to endure discomfort. But she bore value out of a challenge.

Share your knowledge: This is sort of like putting yourself out there, but it is doing a bit more. Here you are positioning yourself either as an expert or a would-be expert in your field through knowledge sharing. You are also sharing your work with people and you have opened an avenue to take feedback for improvement or specialization, in which case, will lead to mastery. If you are a chef for example, you may create a blog or vlog to showcase what you do, if you are a writer, you may share snippets from your upcoming book on your Instagram page. If you are a comedian, you may share some of your contents.

Showing up with value propositions not only puts you out there but also helps people know you and your brand. Remember, the trick to doing this effectively is to be consistent so that your name becomes synonymous with your niche. Of course, this will not happen overnight but with you always sharing your knowledge, you will be attracting the kind of opportunities that will help you meet your goals successfully. It is also important that you are not only sharing your knowledge but also learning new knowledge and sharpening your skills which will help you remain relevant in your sphere.

Have a robust profile: This is an aspect that a lot of people struggle with. Many of us do not know how to build a sellable profile; you have got to be more intentional about it. An idea is to understand that our profiles celebrate our wins and act as a poster for our brand. Take your accomplishments seriously and celebrate every win, it is a big deal. Keep records of accolades won and awards received, track and document every milestone and celebrate even the smallest commendations and compliments. You have earned your stripes and you must wear your badge of honor with pride, this doesn't make you cocky… putting your wins out there helps people remember your feats and recognize that you are a brand.

This is important not just for people who need to know about you but also for yourself, it helps you see your value, boosts your confidence, attracts and prepares you for opportunities. Well, if you do not know who you are, how would you know if other people are accurate in their descriptions of you? Self-awareness is an important skill to master if we must attract opportunities. Saying you helped your organization close an important deal and won an award for it; if you did, it is not bragging. It is simply stating a fact about yourself – it's high time we become comfortable with doing that.

Get a mentor: I have found this to be a very valuable way to attract opportunities. A mentor is available to draw you in, share their life lessons – successes and mistakes – and save you from pitfalls. They can shorten your learning by as much as 5 years. A mentor's perspective can help you skip many steps and put you in the way of opportunities in the shortest time possible. With a mentor, you can gain access to a network and a platform that can speed up your progress towards your goals. You may be introduced to people who are as passionate as you are about your mission and who will open doors that would have been extremely difficult for you to get into. A mentor relationship could also give you access to your ideal clients, who will go on to become loyal customers and people in your corner. You gain access to innovative ways to reach your goals faster, through brainstorming sessions, combined years of experience and exposure that your mentor can guide you with. You can not underestimate the place of a coach/ mentor in your journey.

Listen to people: Meeting people is one way to attract opportunity. You never know how one person will be instrumental to your success. One thing to note when meeting people is to be intentional in getting some useful information about them. It's great to talk about ourselves but you will learn more from others talking about themselves. Learn to ask questions and pay attention when others are speaking. This helps you learn a lot about people, gain new information and have broader perspectives. People are the doors that lead us to our goals; when we listen rather than talk all the time, we can see how we might be aligned. This is not about using people for our personal intentions but about being alert to opportunities that might just be one conversation away.

Get certified in your field: Getting certified is a sure way to inch closer to the opportunities you seek. Not only will getting certified increase your knowledge base. It will boost your confidence and morale towards sharing your knowledge, and it will also boost other people's confidence in your craft. It will attract the kind of clientele that you seek. You will also have more shots coming for collaboration. As you encounter more and more of these opportunities, you will find that you are evolving as a person.

Making The Most of Your Opportunity

Now you have attracted the opportunity you have been waiting for; how do you make the most of it? Below are a few tips to help you.

Recognize and take it: I often hear of young university graduates who are offered a job and they turn it down saying it doesn't meet their requirements in terms of pay and benefits. While the job may not pay you what you believe you deserve, the question to ask is, how much are you currently earning from your efforts? How much job experience do you have? How do you intend to get the job experience required for getting the job you think you deserve, if you do not take the opportunity that finally presents itself to you? According to Thomas Edison, *"Opportunity is missed by most people because it is dressed in overalls and looks like work."* Sometimes we miss great opportunities because they do not look fancy and worthy of our time. Sometimes you want to grow your network and you get invited to an event where you could meet people in your field, yet, you turn it down. That is an opportunity being wasted! I agree you can't say yes to everything, you will burn out; but the question is, are you saying yes enough?

Ask questions: When you now come face to face with what you see as an opportunity, ask questions. Remember, you have done everything to attract this opportunity. Now what looks like an opportunity is in front of you; to make the best of it, ask questions. Is this opportunity in line with your goals? Will it move you closer to where you want to go? Imagine you want to be a writer or an artiste and someone thinks, 'Oh that's such a waste of time, I have a more secure job offer for you.' You want to ask yourself; will this job bring me closer to my dream of becoming a writer or an artiste? If you can work the job and do your writing on the side, or if taking the job will help you grow your network, then it's a great opportunity. If the job will not help you meet the relevant people you should meet or allow you develop your writing or your aspirations on the side, if it takes you further and further away from your goals, then no matter how attractive it looks, you may want to reconsider.

Do a great job: Like Thomas Edison said, opportunities often come looking like work and are dressed in overalls. Sometimes we get the chance to do a job that we have been waiting for but because it may not be a paid opportunity, or we are not paid what we think we deserve, we do a sloppy job thinking that, it doesn't deserve much of our time. In truth, we never know who will see the job done and what recommendations you might get or not get as a result. What I am saying is, whenever we get an opportunity that we have been waiting for, let us give it our best shot. How do you know that someone who will be willing to pay the kind of money you want will not stumble across your work? Would you want them to see the quality of work you have done for free? Do your work like you would if you were presenting it to the most thorough person you know. Do your best. You don't have to be perfect because you may feel cornered to deliver a certain standard, hence, hindering you from making any move and leading to procrastination. Sometimes your best will not be good enough for certain people and that is okay but be sure to constantly improve yourself.

When You Miss An Opportunity

One of the saddest experiences in life is missed opportunities, whether it's a missed job because you did not have the required qualification, or a lost relationship because you were not mature enough. An opportunity is considered lost because you were not prepared, and could not see the value in it.

Whatever it is, missed opportunities are a great source of sadness and sometimes, regret. Having said that, it is not all over for you. If you have lost any opportunity, you can make up for it. You can learn your lessons, move on and go on to smash even bigger goals. What should you do when you realize you have missed an opportunity?

Accept and learn from it: This is the attitude to adopt when you have missed an opportunity even if it was your fault. I saw this quote somewhere as I was doing some research, *"Focusing too much on a lost opportunity can be like carrying around a weight,"* – *Blair Thomas, co-founder of eMerchantBroker.* According to him, carrying too many regrets impacts his ability to see new opportunities. In fact, I dare say, *deadweight,* because it becomes too heavy to move forward with. When we beat ourselves too much over our mistakes, it becomes difficult to move forward. When we miss an opportunity, we must grieve the loss but not for too long. It is more important to understand why we missed the opportunity and restrategize on clinching it another time. Identify what needs to be improved on should you get another opportunity.

Get prepared: Opportunities abound! There will be other opportunities, so you need to equip yourself with the ability to spot those opportunities. Think of what to look out for; what relevant questions should you ask? Think of what you did wrong the first time and make amends, think of things you overlooked that you should pay attention to this time. Do you need to get higher learning? Do you need to practice your craft more? Do you need to be more vocal? What can you do, to ensure you do not miss the next one? – Just be prepared!

Let go of the regrets: Holding on to regrets and the pain of the missed opportunity will make you shut down mentally. You will not be able to access new ideas in your mind. You need to allow yourself space to think creatively and you can only do that by letting go of the regret and the feelings that you failed.

Back to the popular saying I shared with you from my childhood, that an *'opportunity comes but once'*, you can probably now understand why people may think so. Many people do not pick themselves back up after a missed opportunity, instead, they continue to lament about how they missed out on those opportunities. In truth, we are constantly surrounded by opportunities. Let's do some reflection to see if we are putting ourselves in a position to attract opportunity:

- When was the last time you read a book on personal development, finance or something in your field?
- When was the last time you attended a seminar – free or paid?
- When was the last time you volunteered for a cause that interests you – whether related to your field or not?
- When was the last time you did something new for the first time? For example, going to the gym, attending dance lessons, trying a new book...

Every time you take a step forward and do something to gain new knowledge you are opening yourself up for new opportunities. If you have not started, today is a good day to start.

"Change the happenings in your life from obligatory tasks to opportunities for which you are grateful."
- Kathryn Prentice

Think it out loud

- In what ways have you let opportunities pass you by? How did it make you feel?
- What did you do to ensure you made the best use of new opportunities after that?
- What are you doing right now to create opportunities for yourself?

TASK

Make a list of 5 things you can do right now to create opportunities for yourself. Execute one of these plans within the next one week.

Ask someone to hold you accountable.

CHAPTER SEVEN

Networking

"Networking is an investment in your business. It takes time and when done correctly can yield great results for years to come."
- Diane Helbig

A ccording to research, the most successful people are often likewise those who rely heavily on the power of networking.

There was a time I was extremely casual about *networking* because it was something that happened quite naturally for me. I saw it as fun and I looked forward to meeting new people but I never placed any significance to it beyond just that. Of course, looking back now, I realize that my faulty ideas about networking, hindered me from using a very helpful tool to reach my goals.

What does networking mean to you? Do you lean into it or find yourself pulling away from it? In the world we live in, whether it is a business successor relationship or simply a new relationship, we are required to engage in some form of networking. Perhaps, what is hindering you may not be a fear of networking but a fear of what you believe networking to be. So, let us consider what networking is:

What is Networking?

Networking basically comes down to meeting and forming relationships with people for a specific end. Networking could involve exchanging contact information with people who are in a similar field as you. It could also be forming relationships with people so as to create or work on business opportunities. It involves seeking out and sharing information with potential partners.

Networking, however, is not limited to business opportunities or to just people in your field of endeavour. Networking is a skill that can foster a more enriching experience for an individual, as it can be used to build solid lifelong relationships – whether business or casual. Many of the people who are my friends today are people I have met in the course of networking.

Why is Networking Important?

If I had understood earlier the benefits of networking, I definitely would have employed the tool much sooner than I did. Here are some of the reasons why you should consciously make networking a part of your tactics to achieving your goals:

It builds strong business relationships: We have to understand that networking is more about sharing – giving and taking – than it is about just taking. I believe one of the reasons people are averse to networking is because they see it as a selfish act, where people who do not like you pretend to, so as to get business opportunities from you and in a lot of ways, that is how a lot of people see networking. On the flipside, networking is really about engaging your contacts and finding opportunities to help them. By doing this, quite naturally, you will be top of their mind when an opportunity that benefits you comes along.

I have had situations where people will reach out to me with opportunities simply because they know me to be someone who readily shares knowledge and helpful tips. This also works when you are looking for a job, some people will immediately think of you when they see certain job opportunities. Remember, many jobs do not get advertised at certain levels, hence, that is where the power of networking comes in.

New ideas: One way to network that people are not aware of is to join a community. It could be an old school Alumni, a book club, or a business club. As a person of faith, I have found that many people leverage on their church relationships. Being in a church community is amazing but a lot of people in the church community are merely focused on church-based activities. More often than not, they are so engrossed with the church activities that they have little or no time for other things. In some church circles, you might even be shamed for devoting time to anything that is not faith-based, with the argument that the activity lacks spirituality.

Is it any wonder many people of faith struggle with authenticity and fulfilling their dreams as well as making money? When you join a community, your mind is open to new ideas. Please note that, sometimes the ideas come from places or people who are not even in your space or area of work. We cannot overemphasize the place of networking in helping us reach our goals and achieve that dream.

In a community, you have access to people of different backgrounds, experiences and skills to ask for advice. One thing you might encounter is people asking you to pay for advice, what they say is consultancy. While I understand that knowledge is not cheap, I want you to know that there are many others who will gladly share the same information at no cost, especially if you are just starting out. They may recommend a course, a book or some tips to help you. With that, new ideas are birthed, and new viewpoints imbibed. This would not happen without networking.

Gaining new knowledge: Networking opens you up for new learning, which also feeds into new ideas that I mentioned earlier. When you join a community of professionals in your field for instance, you enjoy ease of access to new knowledge – latest techniques, practices and trends in your industry. This will eventually lead you to your goals, whether it is starting and growing a new business or finding a job.

Like I earlier mentioned, it also helps to open your options to people in other industries, there are perspectives they will bring that you may not have had.

Career advancement: Networking the right way brings you visibility, especially in your field. Have you found yourself attending conferences and sometimes bumping into one or two familiar faces? Accessibility is an active advantage in industry networking and it's a door once open, remains open. You realize how small circles get with networking. Even in today's world where virtual activities are the order of the day, it is easy to become more visible. People are often recognized by their given names or social media handles. The more familiar you become with people, the more comfortable you get to offer helpful tips within your community or in the forums you participate in. Also, familiarity and openness allow room for trust. This visibility promotes your reputation as a person of value, and will eventually help to advance your career and achieve your goals, whatever they may be.

Builds confidence: The level of confidence you develop just by putting yourself out there and meeting people is tremendous and immeasurable. By networking, you become more knowledgeable in your field as well as in other areas. By meeting new people and continuing to step out of your comfort zone, you master skills that will serve you in other social and professional circles. There is nothing that builds our confidence like knowing "we can hold our own"anywhere we find ourselves. The better you share your skills with people, the more confident you become.

Build solid relationships: If you ask me, using networking to build relationships is far more important than seeking networking for business. You may disagree with this statement, however, I have found that, even though a networking goal might be to build business relationships and grow businesses, you may actually meet people who become lifelong friends. When someone is your friend, especially if he/she is a trusted friend, it is easier to get them to show you available opportunities than, if you were just a random person they met at a seminar or a conference. As we seek to network to grow our business and reach our life's goals, it is important to be aware that there are other networking opportunities that may not lead to a business deal but will add someone to our inner circle who will be a strong support system.

Hindrances to Effective Networking.

There are only a few people I know personally, who have positive expectations and outcomes about networking. To most of the others, it benefits those who have something to sell or display at an event. These busybodies are perceived as being there to only market their products. When they meet you, they are concerned about what they stand to benefit from you. You hear them go straight to ask questions like – can you come and speak at our event? Can you feature me on your platform? And so on. No plans to gradually get to know you, your needs and what value they can add to you. People like that do not understand what it means to network.

To remove the fear of networking, you have to approach it as though you are bringing value to someone. If you were to offer someone a glass of cold water on a really hot day, would you be afraid that they would think poorly of you? Certainly not! Would you find it easier to say hello to them the next time you see them in a mall or store? Of course!

Networking is that simple. Let us examine reasons why we may have difficulty networking:

Lack of Confidence: Many people who feel they do not have much to offer may feel intimidated reaching out to others. It happens even in connections within a WhatsApp group, where some people will never contribute because they feel they don't know as much as others. These set of people are happy to be observers, and are quick to say, 'we are here to learn'. While there is no harm in learning, everyone has something to share. It is in contributing to discussions that others get to know what value you are adding. Even by asking questions, the conversation can evolve into a reflective moment many times. Just showing up, looking the part and participating is all you need to network. Simply airing your views or even asking questions for clarification is a way of connecting with people. I have helped people begin to change their network and connections just from having simple conversations about their life, their work, which led me to inviting them to my show and meeting people .

It always helps to show up, no matter how fearful you may be.

Inability to Wait: Building a network takes time because it requires building relationships and building relationships take time because they are mostly based on trust rather than by sheer fate of being in a group with an individual. If you attempt to push your business ahead of building your relationship, you might lose the relationship as well as the opportunity for your business. Remember, trust is a currency that takes time to build, it is the virtue of trust that will make your contacts recommend you or your business. You must be willing to dedicate the time it takes to cultivate those friendships.

Wrong Notions: I started out by describing the bias certain people have with regards to networking. Sometimes the confidence with which people network could intimidate you if you do not really understand how it is done. Walking up to someone and launching into business and talking about how you can connect is not networking; it is selling! Networking is more refined. It has to do with you adding value and receiving value in return. If we approach networking as giving value to other people, we will be less nervous about it. It is important to see networking as a win-win rather than it depending on you solely having to market yourself and your products.

Finding Time: One thing that can get in the way of building and leveraging your network is being too busy. Sometimes we can become so bogged down with all the work we do that making time for new networks becomes a chore. It is, however, important to make networking a priority. I mentioned earlier that networking is an open door; one way to keep it forthcoming is to make time. So, you must be deliberate about being available to build new relationships. It is important to note here that not everyone in your network will be on the same degree of closeness. For some people, your relationship will be more about business than anything else while for others, it will be much deeper; and for others still, you will have those who are in your innermost corner. Having this understanding should remove any pressure on our networking agenda, especially as we begin to prioritize growing our craft and reaching our goals above anything else. Have the 'whatever it takes' attitude to making time.

Feeling Inauthentic: Another reason networking is a problem for some people is that they have this idea that there is a networking playbook; and while this may be true to an extent, it is not a one rule fits all. To network successfully, it is more important to be yourself, then adjust the rules to help you along the way. How does a shy person network? There is no way they are going up to a stranger to shake hands and start up a conversation. Finding a way to bring your authentic self into the mix, will definitely help you step out of your comfort zone.

To overcome these hindrances, consider the following:

Rethink Your Beliefs: Always believe you are coming to the table full. You may not have as much as the next person, but you do have something to contribute.

Rethink your fear: What exactly scares you about building a network, meeting people and sharing your thoughts? Invalidate your fear and remember that what you believe is what you will project. Ask yourself why you are more concerned about people's opinions about you? To deal with your fear, you have to revalidate yourself and self-esteem is a good place to start.

Check-ins: A great way to know you have successfully networked is to continue the conversations after the day; however, it is important to note that some people often find it hard to reach out because they don't want to feel like a bother to their contact. So, if your new contacts haven't reached out to you sometime after the event, feel free to check in on them and continue the conversations or exercise new comfort levels with them. Remember, networking is a give and take relationship.

Also, use social media – start by liking a post of someone you feel comfortable with, move on to writing a two-word comment, then start sharing your own views.

Accept rejection: Not everybody will like your comment. How a person responds to what you say, says more about them than it does about you. If you have to shrink back and adjust who you are every time someone criticizes you, who would you become at the end of the day? Many times, the people we are afraid of are struggling with insecurity, and are just projecting the same on us, imagine giving your power away to someone like that.

How then should we network?

If you understand that you are constantly networking, perhaps it will help you be at ease with the idea. The first thing to understand about networking is that it is not about inserting yourself in people's spaces. It is basically getting to know someone better, finding ways to add value to them and also how they can help you too.

Be open to meeting new people through your friends: One of the easiest and least threatening ways to meet people is through friends. Don't shy away from going out with friends and meeting people. You can also meet people at events you organize. When you organize an event, there will be people who will seek you out afterwards; solid relationships have grown from such contacts. When you meet such people, be sure to cultivate the relationship. If you find something that will benefit them, share with them. If you learn of an opportunity they have been looking for, talk to them about it. If you have a question you think they can answer, ask them; that is networking.

I earlier established in chapter five of this book that I remained consistent when people didn't buy my idea, and some left because they didn't see quick results. Another thing I ensured I did was to remain friends with them and maintain a healthy relationship. That they no longer want to be a part of my vision didn't make us enemies, we kept the friendship going. It is amazing that this singular act of maintaining relationships has turned out very beneficial to my business. Although they are no longer on my

A FRIEND CALLED PROCESS

team, they serve as a channel to network and meet new people, build symbiotic, mutually-beneficial relationships, and they patronize and recommend my business.

Use social media: For people who feel intimidated by face-to-face meetings, social media is a great way to meet people and network. It is easy to identify like-minded people. You are likely to find your ideal clients from people you follow on social media. You are prone to become aware of opportunities even by silently following someone on social media. You could then add them to your network or join their community by perhaps buying from them or asking questions about what they do. When you have business to discuss, it becomes a little easier without the pressure of meeting face to face. There are people I have been doing business with that I have never met. I could walk past them on the street and not recognize them, but I can assure you that the relationship is not less beneficial or solid than people that I have business meetings or friendly lunches with.

Don't ask or beg for opportunities: A lot of people think that networking is about asking everyone you meet for a meeting to discuss your business or by exchanging business cards with everyone. I have been at events where before I even got introduced, people had shoved their cards into my hand. I can tell you here that many of those business cards, I never gave a second look. I think it is in poor taste to make it so obvious that you are only interested in pursuing your agenda. A networking event is not merely an opportunity to push your agenda, it is

96

about connecting. Favors can come after the connection door has opened for you, and if done correctly, the conversations go further much quicker and value and virtue is recognized by both parties soon enough.

Make it brief: It is likely that the people you would love to have on your network are busy. With that in mind, keep your interactions brief. Many of us Africans have a way of stretching our greetings. If we are church folks, we have a way of using platitudes that can come across as corny and weathered. Keep your conversations short. There is no need to ask about the welfare of the wife and children, how old they are, how the unstable weather has been to them. There are times when conversations like that will be valuable; when the setting is relaxed. When you meet someone or you are planning to meet someone, always plan ahead what you are going to say. In fact, be the one to hint that you do not wish to take their time (and mean it), they will be more receptive to this.

Let people share their thoughts: I have heard that even when selling, it is a bad idea to just go on talking. This is what a lot of us do. By talking and not allowing your prospect to speak, you are denying yourself the opportunity to know how you may really serve them. One skill that is very important to master in becoming a good conversationalist is the ability to listen and to understand, not to listen to reply. Let me give an example, if you meet someone who you think might be able to provide you some referrals, you could start by asking about their own work, especially if you are in the same industry; you could ask about what struggles they had and how they surmounted it – people like to talk about themselves. Be sure to listen and show interest; asking follow-up questions is a great place to start. If you find a way to insert what you have to share, subtly do it and ask if they know someone who might benefit from it. This removes the pressure from them and they might be more open to it than if you come full force on them.

Gratitude: I have devoted a whole chapter of this book to gratitude. This is because of how important it is. When you show gratitude to people, it leaves a door open that you can walk through another time. Remember that no matter how insignificant you think a person's contribution is to you, there is some value they have added. Always remember to thank them – send an email or a text. Remember this is about building long lasting and authentic relationships that will be mutually beneficial in the end. Do not take for granted whatever information you received. If they speak at your event, thank them, if they give you a slot, thank them, if they gave a recommendation, thank them, even if you didn't get the job or get what you needed. It seems so simple but you will be surprised how many people do not practice this very simple skill. There are people who feel entitled, or do not believe they have to show appreciation for an opportunity because after all, their talent earned them that spot. Stay thankful; wear your gratitude badge, proudly.

As we conclude, it is crucial to mention that no matter your best efforts, some people will not give you the time of day — you are not everyone's cup of tea, as everyone isn't yours either. For reasons best known to them, some people prefer to interact with people on a certain level. So, instead of banging your head against a closed door, leverage on relationships with people who see your worth and appreciate the value you are bringing to them.

Let us do some reflection and tasks to help you get past your fear of networking.

"Pulling a good network together takes effort, sincerity and time."
— Alan Collins

Think it out loud

- Before reading this book, when you heard the word 'Networking' what emotions did it evoke in you? Fear? Disgust? Anger? (Name yours)
- Why did you feel that way? Think of an experience around networking that perhaps triggered that negative feeling.
- Do you think this book has changed your perception about networking? Can you explain how?
- Do you feel more willing to incorporate networking as a tool to growing your business or to helping you reach your goals?

Task

Using the ideas shared in this book, write down the following:

- Three fears you have or had about networking and how you can overcome them.
- Three ways you intend to become more intentional about networking.
- Write down one person who will hold you accountable and support you on this journey.

Reference

Source 1
(https://blog.hubspot.com/marketing/networking-quotes)

CHAPTER EIGHT

Influence

"Influence is when you are not the one talking and,
yet your words fill the room; when you are absent
and yet your presence is felt everywhere."
— Temitope Ibrahim

Growing up, did you hear statements about somebody being a bad influence on others? Did you hear words like 'ringleader'? Maybe you were the 'ringleader', or you were the one accused of being a bad influence. Maybe in class, your keenness to take the lead made people call you a know-it-all. Have you unconsciously imbibed the belief that it is better to stay in the background because of this? In the course of working with people over the years, I have seen extremely brilliant people slink into the background.

At meetings, they rarely contribute and hold back on their opinions and questions; they are content with simply doing what they are told, often to avoid dredging up old triggers. So many gifted people shrink their personality because they are afraid of being called proud; they are afraid of bringing any form of attention to themselves, to avoid being accused of trying to take over leadership.

Growing up those years, in Nigeria, it was not normal as a child to raise questions with your superiors, for fear of embarrassing them, especially if they didn't have the answers. When you were asked 'why did you do such and such', it was more of a rhetorical question than it was any interest in understanding your reasons or knowing your thoughts.

You were more likely to receive a slap for answering back if you dared to respond, as you would be deemed rude. Then, it was seen as part of the greater African discipline but I believe the relationships are improving now. Then, you couldn't ask a grown-up '*why*?' Because asking 'why?' meant you were challenging authority or you were just rebellious or troublesome.

One of the key qualities of a leader or anyone who seeks to wield positive influence is to solve problems; and a key element of problem-solving is the ability to ask appropriate questions and to answer or get the answers from those asked – two very vital skills that many people struggle to demonstrate.

So, what does the word influence immediately mean to you? What emotions does it evoke in you? How comfortable are you being a source of influence? These are questions we must ask and answer if we will reach our goal of being successful in our endeavor. Every interaction you have, even your attitude towards people, has the potential to influence you in ways that you cannot imagine. This is something to think deeply about, as it could be the difference between making the impact that you have been desiring and staying stuck.

The meaning of influence

Being influential is being able to have an effect on the thoughts and perhaps behavior of another person. Influence goes beyond telling people what to do. You could tell people what to do and they would do it until they are out of your sphere of influence. Generally, people are influenced by the music they listen to, books they have read, other people's philosophy of life and these are influences carried on for years or even decades, and they are passed on from generation to generation. Influence is about understanding yourself and how you impact people.

Most people do not realize it, but there is an impression people have about us whether we are quiet, visible or not. Often, this impression determines how they relate with us and how much influence we have over them. Many of us, like I earlier mentioned, have amazing gifts that we can share with the world, but we fail to use these gifts in our network; thus, failing to influence those around us, leading to poor leadership and a lack of influence.

It is important to understand that the extent to which you can help people or get support from others is determined by how much influence you wield over them. To be a person of influence does not mean you have to lord it over people; sometimes, the lack of understanding about what it means to be a person of influence makes us shy away from this very important task. There is a lot of creativity and talent waiting to be expressed and there are so many people who are stuck waiting to receive insight from us. We must be willing to step up, into our place of influence if we will be a blessing to our world. Influencing involves listening carefully, being non-threatening, which earns you actual respect. It involves seeing the other person's perspective and adopting them, which makes it easy for them to adapt to you as well. Many people who find themselves in leadership positions whether they are aware of it or not, demonstrate these skills.

There are many ways we can influence people. Dan Black, highlights four ways our influence can be felt. (Source 1), these are:

Negative influence: This type of influence as he says is the most damaging. It is wielded by leaders who lack the ability to get genuine followership. These leaders are often prideful and leave organizations reeling from the effect of poor productivity and even toxicity.

Neutral influence: This type of leader is what we call, in my local parlance 'short one', meaning the group is short by one. In other words, they might as well not be present, they do not add or take away from the group. They have the title, get the check but do not do the work. Being proactive or taking the lead is not their strength. These are typically those who like to be the nice guys.

Positive influence: This type of influence comes from leaders who add value and leave people better than they found them. This type of influence is the type where people are led actively, leaders are proactive about envisaging problems and leading actively to find solutions. Leaders here are often proactive. Here, relationships are consciously built, and leaders are intentional about the influence they wield.

Life changing influence: This is the highest and most valuable form of influence. This type of influence takes time to build and reaches vast numbers of people. It brings about life changing transformation that remains long after the influencer has left the organization or even passed on. You may have worked in an organization that long after the leader left, there were still strong reminders that such a person passed through your organization, perhaps because of the company culture that he or she re-engineered. The person may have left the company but their influence lives on; that is a life changing influence.

Importance of influence

Your ability to influence people can be the difference between an effective working environment and a non-productive one. Influence results to achieving results quicker or not or even the ability to empower or disempower people around you. Influence is often wrongly perceived as imposing personal will on others through coercion, but in fact, it is a subtler impact. When we learn to be positive influencers, we will become more effective leaders in our homes, workplaces and wherever we find ourselves, and this skill is a must if we are to reach our goals. Your ability to influence is what will make people buy into your vision and help you achieve it.

Why is influence important? Below are a few reasons:

Win others over: When you influence people, remember you are getting them to see your perspective in a non-threatening manner. This may take longer to achieve but is more sustainable in the long run. When we coerce people to do what we want, whether as parents, teachers, bosses or any other authority figure, we may achieve results in the short term, but it will be more difficult for us to sustain the tempo as we will always need to use force or threat to achieve it. This will wear us out. Having influence means having the ability to get people to come with you on a journey willingly because you are able to win their support. This is a key skill to possess as a leader.

Easier to build a team: As earlier mentioned, a person who wishes to make a positive influence seeks others' opinion about a task that they would be involved in. It is a lot easier to get everyone you will be working with, whom you have certain expectations of, on board. It helps that they know what your expectations are and how they can support you. It is erroneous thinking that being tough will make it easier to get people to do your bidding, and as earlier mentioned, while that is possible in the short term, it is unsustainable in the long term. Human capital is a very important factor of production, this is what drives the other factors of production, so you want to make sure you have put together a very good team to help you drive your goals. If you are able to work well with others, you will be a person of influence and will no doubt get to your goals faster.

Impact leadership: If your goal is to make a difference as a leader, you must master the skill of influencing others. Your ability to influence others is the difference between making the impact you want and getting a negative outcome. Influence is so powerful that you can get people who are completely opposed to you to begin to work for your benefit and accelerate movement within the circles that already understand your vision. Influence cannot be overemphasized in leadership and in achieving your personal goals.

Influence is so important that even in trying times, you can get your team to stick with you. I must mention at this point that it is important to have people around you when you reach your finish line. If by the time you reach your goals, everyone who started with you have all left or possibly, you find out you really have no-one in your corner, it might be an indication that you are lacking influence. If you have a message you want to share with the world, how many people can you reach all by yourself?

This is where the people you have influenced come in, they will run with your vision and share this message to places that would have been impossible for you to reach.

What areas can I wield influence?

At this point, you are feeling like you are now ready to be a person of influence but you are not sure in what capacity to function. There are so many ways we can be people of influence. These include; being an attentive parent, a kind neighbor, an empathetic colleague... We do not need a large platform to have a voice or use it. There are other ways we can influence our communities. Take my charity organization for example, we are focused on the Black Ethnic Minority in Scotland. I also have a faith-based outreach where I wield a lot of influence, and to give more clarity, take a moment to consider the seven spheres of influence.

Always remember that each sphere can be influenced either for good or bad. You can use your influence in the following areas:

- Government/ Politics
- Economy; in the areas of science, technology and business
- You could show up as a faith-based outreach, there is a tremendous amount of influence in this area and this is an opportunity to influence mindsets
- Education is a vast space to use your influence
- Family

- Media
- And of course, in Arts such as Sports and Entertainment.

The world is waiting for you, your community is waiting for you, your family is waiting for you. You must begin to show up now! (Source 2)

Seeing how vast the space for influence is, there is so much work to be done. Education for instance can be used as a tool to reverse negative mindsets, unhealthy and unhelpful cultural beliefs. Combining education with Arts over time has shown a massive and helpful shift in thinking, which is evidenced in attitudes and behaviour.

Why are certain nations known to be very neat, others very hardworking and disciplined, yet others permissive, corrupt or repressive? It's all about influence – what kind of education are the citizens of those nations getting? What do they glorify in their entertainment – movies and music? What do their religious leaders focus their teaching on? What is the quality of family life? It would greatly help to pay attention to these areas and you would see the root cause of any country's problem or the reason for their success.

Why people shy away from influencing others.

Seeing how much room there is to influence our world, we must become more intentional about seizing every opportunity to wield influence, starting with ourselves and our immediate community. There is however, one thing that sometimes is an obstacle to this, and that is the fear of influence itself. A good number of people are ever ready with excuses for why they cannot be more involved in their community; I dare say, these excuses are mostly selfish. As people would rather have others take the lead on such, while they come in as support – hence, playing a more passive than active role. While none of this is bad, it is important for people to begin to see their life purpose as a responsibility to the world and become bolder in achieving it.

First thing to do is remove the fear of being seen as a manipulator or a pushy person. This is one reason certain people keep quiet and hide their gifts; fear stifles our ability to think or act rationally or creatively. It is generally more difficult to break out and follow the road less traveled in situations like this, for fear of being ostracized; hence, people would rather keep quiet than risk being called a control freak, a manipulator or a fraud.

We must understand that sometimes fear is conjured in our minds as what we tell ourselves will happen if we attempt certain things or behave in a particular way. More often than not, many things we fear never come to pass and if they do, we are usually able to cope and manage them better than we imagined. To become a person of influence, we must tackle fear or else, we will not get started and will stop pursuing our goals, if at all we do get started. If you feel unqualified or bear some impostor syndrome, it is a justifiable and popular enough reason for why so many people don't step up to tasks. With impostor syndrome, people believe they are not educated enough, they are not from the right community, they do not have the right backgrounds, they are not qualified or talented enough… We must rid ourselves of the thought that we must be bigger than we are to become influential. Many of us carry way more influence than we realize. Sometimes, all it takes is asking the right questions, sometimes it is sharing our stories, but it starts with us believing that *we are* and *can be* people of influence.

How can you be a person of influence?

There is so much talk about influence and leadership that sometimes, it can become just another word being thrown around; but it is important to understand that one of the ways to live a meaningful life is to walk in your influence. As earlier mentioned, you need to first see yourself as a person with something to give, a purpose to share and then the influencer in you can surface. Anyone can influence another, the question is how positively or negatively can this happen? If you do nothing and stay in the shadows, even that in itself is a statement; it is saying to others that you value your comfort over and above everyone and anything else.

It is somewhat understandable that you would want to be neutral in such an unpredictable world, however, aloof never makes influence or impact. No purpose is achieved with a neutral position. Let your purpose create an interference design, where you damn all critics and naysayers and share your gift with the world, starting with the community you live in. Serve from where you are, and yes, do it afraid! Get the support, training you need but do it. The opportunities are endless, you just need to be willing to look inwards for a purpose-driven inspiration, instead of out, to the loud distractions of critics.

To become a person of influence, there are certain traits one must possess. Below are a few of them:

Integrity: In the early 2000's, I became aware of the Multi-Level Marketing business (popularly called MLM). It was common to hear people talking about this business idea and wanting to recruit level agents. Once you joined their network, you would become wealthy and travel all over to many parts of the world, as level rewards.

The catch was this: *You'd never have to work for the rest of your life*. The only problem was many of the people who preached this message had not experienced what they were selling to you. Soon, I realized that it was indeed possible to become wealthy and travel like they told me, this, however, required hard work and consistency – now that part was not sold at recruitment level, you had to buy in to figure it out or just have your wits up to catch the con. Let me explain this - the people who were trying to sell to me had not achieved the success they were talking about, some of them were still fairly new in the business and were just enthusiastic sales people at best. They had no clue what it took to get to the outcome they were talking about.

When you do not have any personal experience to show people, it will be hard for you to influence anyone. There are people who believe in the 'fake it till you make it' syndrome, well hopefully, you won't be exposed while you are still faking it. When people do not see a connection between who you are and what you portray yourself to be, you will not be able to influence them. You must be a person of integrity to be a person of influence.

If you are a parenting coach who has had issues with your children and you overcame them, you are more likely to influence other parents by sharing your struggles than if you simply portray yourself as the perfect human and parent who has always known what to do. It is a known fact that nobody is perfect, and there is no training for perfection, either. As an authenticity coach, I share my stories of times when I used to go with the crowd because I believed that was what was expected. My effectiveness comes from my vulnerability; that is where the influence is.

Connection: Connectors make natural influencers because they are open-minded, empathetic and are able to see the viewpoints of other people. They may disagree sometimes, but because of their natural disposition to people, they usually have a broad perspective because of their willingness to consider diverse thoughts and opinions. They are not afraid to adjust or change their views if they see superior arguments or evidences to show that they may not be correct. This quality allows them to identify what people need and it makes it easier for them to influence people. People are more likely to follow you, if you can touch their heart. Influence is more emotional than rational. How you communicate your points is crucial for any level of connection. It takes a certain level of self-awareness to know what to say and to say it in a way to get the right attention. According to Voltaire, *"The ear is the avenue to the heart."* Having said that, balance is important, so you don't become overly focused on diplomacy or political correctness so much that you lose the essence of your message.

Boldness: Not everyone who has a huge following wields positive influence or has a helpful message but what is common to all individuals with influence is their boldness. To be a person of influence is to be a person of courage; you must be bold to speak your truth. If you do not speak up, it will not matter what awesome opinions and thoughts you have inside of you. So, show up and be consistent. Like I earlier mentioned, people today are very hostile to those who do not believe what they believe; you are susceptible to their judgment and attack for not standing with their opinions or perceptions. It is even more scary if you feel you might be going against popular opinion. There is the tendency to remain quiet and go with the flow and that means we will be giving up our opportunity to stand in a position of influence. Sometimes, the people you are seeking to influence are authority figures, it takes a certain amount of courage to do that.

Get training: Influence is something that can be learned, be it formally or informally. Some skills that are relevant to becoming a person of influence are picked up as we pursue our dreams. One could pick up communication skills from talking about their business; it is also possible to understand people's needs through interactions with them. However, for formal training in a specific sphere of influence, you may want to formally enrol for a training course – for example, if you want to have influence in the movies, you will need to train on movie production, script writing, and possibly learn how the industry works in order to use it to your full advantage.

As I conclude, think about how you can begin to influence the world around you. Start from where you are!

"Never underestimate the influence you have on others."
– Laurie Buchanan

Think it out loud

- What does the word Influence mean to you?
- What feelings are evoked in you when you think of being a person of influence?
- If negative, from where do you think you first developed those negative feelings?
- Did you know before now that you are or could be a person of influence?
- If you didn't, what does the realization mean to you?
- In what ways do you find taking the lead challenging?
- What do you think hampers you from being a person of influence?
- What two things do you think you can start doing today to move you closer to being a person of influence?

Reference

Source 1 -
(http://danblackonleadership.info/archives/6731)

Source 2
(https://shoremount.kayako.com/article/43-what-are-the-seven-spheres-of-society)

A FRIEND CALLED PROCESS

CHAPTER NINE

Empowering Others

"There will be many people whose lives you have enriched
who may never tell you it – or that you've never even met –
but you will have enriched them nonetheless."
- Rasheed Ogunlaru

One of the ways to build lasting influence and to successfully reach your life's goals is through people empowerment. To empower, by definition, means to put power or to give power to something or someone. Empowering people therefore means helping people achieve their goals, enabling people perhaps by teaching them a skill or creating an enabling environment for them to achieve their goals.

To empower someone is to give them wings to fly, it is to show them how competent they are. It is to help build their self-esteem, or to show them their potential and how to maximize it. It is not to give them fish but to teach them to fish. When a person is empowered, they become independent and are able to stand on their two feet and pursue their dreams. Can I ask you this question? Who have you been empowering?

Why you should empower others

I once saw an article with a screaming opening statement which I will summarize; *"I hate the word empowerment. I never think I should empower anyone"*. I found myself wondering about it as I continued reading the article, it soon became clear what this writer meant. In the writer's opinion, empowering people meant that they needed our permission, our influence or our gifts to achieve their goals. He believed that people are inherently gifted and all we need to do is help them harness their gifts and get out of their way.

We could create the best environment for them to come to the realization of who they are, as well as how gifted they are, then hands off for them to reach their goals, thereafter. I want to say that empowerment denotes different things and the writer described a very important way we can help people thrive. I personally do not believe that to empower a person means they need my permission for anything; it does mean that my influence in their lives should be such that they achieve their goals and though it might require some hand-holding to guide them because not everyone has clarity regarding their goals in life.

Empowerment should lead to independence, as it is to help them see their innate ability and to help them in some cases make the right decisions about honing their skills in areas where they fall short. In a recent research by Jay A. Conger, author *Leadership: The Art of Empowering Others,* shows that with sharing of power comes more productivity. He also believes that the notion that leaders must guard their power is outdated and therefore ineffective. To empower a person is a great act of courage on the part of the leader and kindness to the person being empowered.

Let us examine a few reasons why it is important to empower people:

Phenomenal personal and professional growth in people: One of the things I have observed in all my time in my workplace is, the leaders who are in touch with their team members usually get the most out of their staff. That is not to say, there won't be one person who just refuses to work with you, but generally, it is easier to get people to be on your side when you empower them. This is because when you create an enabling environment for people to thrive, it allows them to dig deep and find capabilities to deliver more excellently. Many times, they surprise themselves at how competent they get; this awareness increases their confidence which translates to higher productivity, very much to their own delight.

Positive Energy: One of the complaints people have when they are in a group is the feeling of being side-lined. In an organization where people don't feel they are heard, there is bound to be a lot of toxicity, which will undermine their work quality. When people feel like their contributions are appreciated, it is easier for things to be done. People who feel empowered feel a connection to the person or a sense of duty to the organization that empowers them. They understand and appreciate their role because it has been communicated clearly, leaving them feeling confident that they can share their concerns and get the support they need, should the need arise. In an environment like this, productivity is enhanced.

Transition to leadership is easy: Transition to leadership is easy when people are involved in processes in your organization and are allowed to make decisions to a certain degree. People generally do better when they feel that the leadership trusts them. Hence, mistakes should be a learning ground without the fear of harsh criticism; with this, they become more competent and will find transition to leadership easier. Even in the family life with our children, it is easier to get your child to come home at an agreed time if they know you are banking on them to keep the trust. In empowering people, you are passing the baton of leadership and helping them see their own value through your lens.

Why people are reluctant to empower others

A long time ago, I read a funny post (I can't even remember the source). It was a conversation between the CEO of a company and the CFO about training the staff. The details are a little sketchy now but the CFO wanting to save money said, "Well, what if we train the staff and they leave us to our competitors?" The CEO responded, "What if we don't train them and they stay?!"

Refusing to empower your staff will cost you more in the long run. It is in our best interest to empower those who work for and with us. The truth is empowerment cuts across many levels: family, work, community… and in these spheres, we have the opportunity to empower or disempower people. We empower our children when we teach them to be independent; doing everything for them may seem easier; yet, in the long run, the quick-fix solutions become a burden not just for us but for them as well because, they will struggle to find their feet when life throws its curve balls at them, having never learned the skills to thrive.

Why then are people reluctant to empower others in spite of the benefits?

Fear: During the slave era, there was an Anti-literacy Law which forbade slaves to be taught to read and write. The fear was borne out of the fact that if the slave became enlightened, they would no longer be content with their situation and would revolt against it. There were fears that slaves could forge documents required to escape to free states, so there was a law to disempower them. A few of my friends who are school teachers in different parts of Africa often tell me that many school owners refuse to train their teachers; reason being, what if we train them and they leave? With this mentality, it is little wonder that a lot of these schools are filled with teachers who do not have the requisite skills to properly develop the children in their care.

It may seem like a short-term win for the school, however, with time, the quality of education drops and the damage becomes deep-seated. This, together with many other factors, could cripple the productive capacity of any nation; sadly, some people in authority want to keep it that way because then they can control others.

Many managers fear to acknowledge their staff for a job well done, so instead they keep quiet about the individual's contributions, or even go on to act like it was due to their influence or support that the person was able to deliver such an outstanding job. In the same way, such leaders will have no problem throwing their staff under the bus even if the mistake was due to their own bad judgement. This attitude stems from a feeling of fear and threat to their position, so they do anything to keep people down.

Lack of trust: Sometimes, when we do not empower people, it may be due to our desire to always be in control of decisions because we believe we are the only ones who can do the right thing. People who are perfectionists tend to fear delegating to others, they tend to be unable to trust anyone to do it like they would. They would hire smart people, yet, leave them with organizational stunted growth. Lack of trust could be due to the leader's personality or perhaps due to a bad experience. The fact that somebody he empowered may take a decision that can cost the organization, for which he might have to account for, could certainly make him reluctant to give that level of control. It takes a lot of courage to let people under your leadership make certain decisions at times.

Laziness: Once, at a parenting seminar, I heard someone describe a parenting style as *'lazy parenting'*, this is a situation where there is no intentionality on the part of the parent. There is no dialoguing or being firm, it is either the extreme of crushing every dissent with force or just letting the children do as they please. To empower people requires deep thinking and planning, for a clear strategy on how to help people grow. It requires intentionality – checking on progress and providing intervention to move people from one point to another. It takes work, work which many leaders may not be ready to put in.

How to empower people?

When you think of empowering others, consider it as empowering yourself. How do you empower yourself? You probably have a goal; hence, you must put a strategy in place to measure your progress and evaluate your strategy from time to time. That is the same way you empower people. Empowering people is deliberate and that is why it is such a difficult task for people to embark on and why mentors are such an invaluable resource. How then, do we empower others?

Identify the people you want to empower

Not everyone will have the opportunity to lead a team in the workplace, however, everyone has a sphere of influence that they can play in, even children if we show them how. There are several spheres we can empower people in; you can empower your family members and close friends, you can empower your colleagues even if you are not the boss and you can empower people in your community – your neighbors and people you generally come in contact with. Empowering your children, for instance, requires you to share your family values with them and help them imbibe the same; more importantly, is to love them and allow them to be heard and seen. In the workplace, recognizing your colleagues and appreciating what each person brings to the table, can be empowering.

People make the mistake thinking they do not have to show their appreciation to others, that would be a grave mistake. Sometimes, it is the thought that we are making an impact that keeps us going and we may not know if no one tells us. In my business for instance, we empower ourselves by reading books, enrolling for relevant courses, in-house training, and knowledge sharing. In your community, you can find a need and meet it. Start a reading club or teach life skills. There are many opportunities through which you can empower others, but the most important person to empower is yourself; you cannot pour from an empty cup.

Get your team and management support
As important as it is to empower people, people may resist it. I have heard people make comments at training events such as *'Let's just drink their coffee and go back to work'*, without coming to the full realization of what it cost the company to put the training together. I have also found out that sometimes people are sent

for training in areas that do not necessarily benefit them, it is HR merely ticking the boxes. To prevent this situation, let the process be clear and transparent; whatever form of empowerment you are offering, ensure they see the full benefits and understand why they should actively participate.

A more ideal situation is to ask people what areas they think they require support. Ask them what their goals are, with respect to their key (job) objectives; this helps them see that you are interested in them and will encourage them to start thinking intentionally about their life's purpose and goals. They may need your help identifying their goals because some people may have difficulty identifying or articulating their needs. It is also possible they might need your support to understand that empowerment is not done without carefully thought out plans, and ensuring everyone is on the same page.

Be as positive as possible

I once saw a post that said *'To empower means to put power into, as well as to bring enthusiasm out of '*. I love that definition. Attitude is contagious. A friend once relayed her experience while still in full time employment; she worked at an international company that she really loved, the energy was positive, and everyone worked like a team until she got a new line manager.

She told me, she noticed that from the very first week he joined, he was quite critical of people that he barely knew and before long, the company became a toxic place. Interestingly, this person in question had a charming personality, so people did not exactly realize what was happening because unintentionally, he created a blend of criticism and charisma – hence, a contagious positive energy was also spreading.

Another way to empower people is to let them know you are always dependable. One of the most charming qualities of a leader is the ability to stay calm in the midst of a crisis. This quality like no other is capable of holding the team together because people tend to look to their leaders for support in times like this. Our attitude as leaders will determine the atmosphere in our organization. Another way to show positivity is to appreciate those who work with us, it helps them see that they are valuable. Be conscious of people's need for affirmation, and try not to hurt their self-esteem. These are really simple things to do but surprisingly, are lacking in a lot of workplaces.

Do as you expect

A very good example of where this can be demonstrated is the home. Often as parents, we tend to tell our children how to behave when sometimes our own behavior doesn't match our words. To empower people, we must *show* them how to behave. Do you want people to hand in quality work? Then ask yourself, what quality of work are you doing? Do you want them to be punctual? Also, ask, are you punctual to work? If you want your team to embrace a specific behavior, the easiest way to get them to imbibe it, is for them to see you do the same. You could coerce and threaten with queries and punishment, but it is more effective to lead by example.

Allow creativity and independence

Micromanaging people disempowers them. Constantly checking, criticizing, correcting and even blaming does not help the team's esteem. As leaders, we should give people the power to make certain decisions. Our job should be more of a coach. Allowing your team some measure of autonomy is a key element to empowering them. The trust makes it easier for them to perform; this encourages self-motivation and self-discipline, and will create an environment where people thrive and become more productive.

Be their cheerleader

People around us go through different phases in life just as we do. One way of empowering people is to help them develop a sense of confidence in you; to make them understand that regardless of their circumstances, you will cheer them on. Many times, people refuse to attempt new tasks or take the initiative for fear that if they fail, they will be harshly criticized; empowering such people would mean letting them know that you trust them to make the right decisions and that they have your support regardless of the outcome.

It does not mean, however, that an unreliable team member with a track record should be ignored; such a person should be given little autonomy, until they have proven themselves repentant.

Important to note, learn to applaud and reward winners and all who excel. That is what it means to invest in a person.

"As we look ahead into the next century,
leaders will be those who empower others."
— *Bill Gates*

Think it out loud

Here are a few questions to reflect upon:

- What is the most empowering experience you have ever had?
- In what ways do you think you have empowered the people around you?
- In what ways do you think you can begin to empower people around you?

TASK

Here is one thing you can do immediately to put these ideas into action.

Look for ways to make people feel appreciated. Remember it could be your family and friends and colleagues and of course your subordinates. Help people see how valuable they are.

CHAPTER TEN

Gratitude

*"I've had a remarkable life. I seem to be in such good
places at the right time. You know, if you were to ask me
to sum my life up in one word, gratitude."*
- Dietrich Bonhoeffer

Y̶ou might be at a point in your life where you feel there
is nothing to be grateful for. Perhaps you have bills that
are mounting so high, perhaps your marriage has fallen
apart, perhaps you have lost a loved one, perhaps you lost your
job because of the pandemic or maybe, you have lost your home
and now you have to move back home with your parents... It
can be hard to feel grateful when life seems to be out to get you.

Can I ask you to be patient with me as I show you what gratitude
means to me and why you should consider embracing a life of
giving thanks?

There is a lot that I aspire for, I cannot say, I have reached all my
goals, or that I have achieved the success that I am aiming for.
I can say this for a fact, I am in a much better place than I was

five (5) years ago; I am in a better place, mentally, than I was last year. With this, I can confidently say I now have the skills I need to navigate my circumstances and reach the results I need.

I find that every time I pause to think about all the good that has happened to me, even the tiniest good, I feel energized and I receive the strength to continue. Gratitude has helped me a great deal to overcome my low moments and to prevent me from spiralling into a dark place. Your story may be different from mine, you might be in a worse place than you were last year, but can I ask you to pause a little and look inwards; do you have any skills? Do you have any talent? Do you have any useful knowledge? Do you have a friend? Can you put all of these together and make even the tiniest movement forward? If you have at least one of these, there is hope, and you do have something to be grateful for.

Gratitude is that feeling of being thankful and that readiness to be appreciative even of the littlest thing. Sometimes people feel a little miffed when asked to be grateful because they think you are asking them to accept an inferior life. Being thankful has nothing to do with accepting mediocrity and being unmotivated, it is taking stock of our lives and seeing that we have what it takes to move us towards our life goals, as well as, acknowledging the good that is in our lives. Remember, being grateful should not only be for things that we see, which is what we tend to focus on. Everything we have, both tangible and intangible, are gifts and deserve gratitude; and if we are grateful for them, our ability to maximize them increases and this helps us move toward our goals.

Importance of gratitude

Gratitude helps people feel more positive emotions: When you focus on what is good in your life, you are more likely to be uplifted. I have heard people say, *'what you focus on, increases.'* I know this to be true, as even in my life, whenever I choose to focus on the good that is in my life regardless of whether I am achieving all my goals or not, I find that I begin to see more opportunities and more possibilities. Many new ideas have been birthed just by focusing on the good that I already have. A research conducted by two psychologists, Dr. Robert A. Emmons and Dr. Michael E. McCullough, involved three groups of participants where they asked participants to write a few sentences a week on particular topics.

One group wrote about things they were grateful for, the other group wrote about everything that upset and irritated them and a third group wrote about stuff that affected them without assigning a positive or negative label to it. It was discovered that the group that focused on what they were grateful for, appeared to have a better quality of life, they worked and had fewer visits to the doctor. (Source 1) Even though there are exceptions to this, there are people who may utter words of gratitude but feel no different. In truth, regardless of how much we hear it or even how much we might have benefited from showing gratitude in the past, we may currently or temporarily not feel grateful, and that is okay but gratitude has been shown to impact positively on well-being and it is something to consider when we feel like there is nothing good going on with us.

Gratitude can improve relationships: How do you feel towards people who are generally thankful and who show appreciation? Yes, you feel drawn to them. Of course, people can be overly effusive that it comes across as insincere, but I am referring to a heartfelt 'thank you' that comes from a place of true appreciation. Everybody likes that. Who doesn't like the boss that says 'Well done team'? Who doesn't want to do more for the spouse that says, 'Thank you'?

Gratitude, no matter how small, is a wonderful tool to propel us towards our life's goals. Gratitude enhances connection and satisfaction in our friendships and romantic relationships. If you want your relationships to last, embrace gratitude; eschew entitlement. As a Christian I am reminded of the story of Jesus and ten lepers, who had come to him for healing and only one came back to say, 'Thank you', even Jesus, was appreciative of the gesture and from the story, you could tell that the act of coming back to show appreciation, sealed that leper's blessing. Indeed, the Bible is filled with admonishments to Christians to be thankful, and offer thanksgiving always, even in difficult circumstances – there must be something about gratitude that is deeply beneficial.

Gratitude improves your health: According to several research works, being grateful can improve your sleep, and reduce stress by helping you manage stressors more effectively and even decrease depression while improving your heart condition. (Source 2) Sleep conditions we know are connected to heart conditions. Many times, when we are unable to sleep, it is probably because we are dealing with some angst, which comes from negative thoughts. Being grateful means that we are choosing to focus on more positive possibilities and less negative possibilities; which means that there is less pressure and the possibility of better sleep and overall better health. Do you know that if you are stressed or in poor health, you will not be able to think creatively and that will definitely affect your goals? We cannot underestimate the place of appreciation in achieving our life's goals.

Why is gratitude hard for people?

Having seen some of the benefits of gratitude, it would be good to understand why some people find it hard to show appreciation to themselves or others.

Entitlement and Self-absorption: When a person feels that they deserve more, they will not show appreciation. I read a post on Instagram where a young man was complaining about a friend of his who had asked him for money. He immediately counted ₦20,000 (Naira) and gave it to him but the friend said something to the effect of, 'a big boy like you should be able to give more than this.' To which the man asked his friend to return the money and send his account details so he could send him ₦100,000. The friend indeed returned the money, and according to the writer, his friend is still waiting for the money as he has since blocked him on his phone. Why do we sometimes believe people owe us? When people feel like they deserve more, they will not show appreciation. This is also called the entitlement mentality.

Envy: Many times, we deprive ourselves of the joy of enjoying what we have because we lack something that another person has. Envy is quite subtle, and far more people demonstrate envy than they care to admit. When we find ourselves feeling resentful because of another's possessions or the quality that we lack, we will find it difficult to be grateful. You may find yourself suddenly feeling discontent simply because your friend or colleague now has what seems to you like an advantage over you. To be stuck in a place of envy is to be stuck in ingratitude, and this will snuff out our joy. I often hear people say, when God wants to bless you, He blesses someone close to you, so He can see your reaction. I don't know where that saying came from, but the truth is, if you can be happy for your friend or colleague, you will likely be more motivated to succeed in life, rather than stewing in your envy which can keep you down for a long time.

Expectations: Have you ever found yourself reminding your teenage child to show appreciation for something you bought them or did for them? Do you find yourself not showing appreciation for a gift from your spouse or for a task they helped you complete? We can become so used to expecting certain things to be done for us that we lose sight of the need to be grateful. Yes, there are certain expectations we have of people and which might not be a big deal when they do it, but whether we show appreciation or not, reflects who we are. It doesn't mean we are bad people; indeed, we could become forgetful due to being used to receiving from people close to us. The danger however is, we may burn our relationships and become people who are difficult to be around.

Lack of awareness: We often underestimate the effect of showing appreciation to the giver. Showing our appreciation has a very positive impact on the donor or giver; oftentimes, we are unaware of this and may assume they do not mind us being ungrateful. Some people might say, 'I don't need to show I am grateful, they ought to know that I appreciate what they have done.' No, that's not good enough. Someone shared a conversation with a friend who was upset about his wife's sudden hostile attitude. He had lost his job and his wife had stepped up to hold the forte. He often told his friends how when he became rich, he would show his wife how thankful he was, but he never voiced it out to her, nor did he even try to support her at home. He assumed just feeling grateful in his head was enough. Of course, his wife started to feel used and unappreciated and he didn't understand why.

How to be more grateful.

Reflect on where you are: It is very likely that you may not have achieved all your goals, but you are not where you started. You may have made new friends, and learned more. You may have become more mature and learned to overcome your grief. When we learn to reflect on our lives, we think about obstacles we have surmounted and remember how everything always works out and even how far we have come; then we are well on our way to becoming more grateful.

Be careful what you say: Negative talk can keep us in a loop. If you are focused on things that have gone wrong and continue going on about how difficult life is, gratitude becomes harder. And when we are not grateful, we notice fewer things to be grateful for. As a person, I am constantly looking for little things to be thankful for, and because I am always in my gratitude mode, I seem to attract something more to be grateful for.

Count your blessings: There is a song I remember every time I talk about gratitude, 'Count your blessings, name them one by one.' It is useful to keep a gratitude journal, where we can periodically enter specific things we are grateful for. As a person of faith, I start my prayers every day with thanksgiving. I must admit, sometimes, I fall into a routine and do not exactly pay attention but it is a healthy practice to have – to daily count your blessings and name them, you will be amazed at how much good there is in your life and this can make you more hopeful and thus, attract what you want.

As we conclude, what are you grateful for? Think about this and let your heart take stock and be grateful.

"Gratitude turns what we have into enough."
— Anonymous

TASK

Get a journal, you can call it a gratitude journal.

At the end of the day, enter 5 things that made you smile, and that you were thankful for.

Read the five things from the previous day in the morning and look out for anything you can be grateful for – Five things every day.

REFERENCES

Source 1
(https://www.health.harvard.edu/healthbeat/giving-thanks-can-make-you-happier)

Source 2
(https://chopra.com/articles/6-proven-benefits-of-gratitude)

A FRIEND CALLED PROCESS

Conclusion

In these ten chapters, we considered your life's purpose and how to discover it. We looked at authenticity and the role it plays in helping you reach your goals. We looked at the importance of gaining new knowledge and going on to master your craft. We considered why being consistent is a must if you are to succeed. We dwelt on the importance of creating opportunities and being open and ready to take advantage of opportunities.

We looked at networking and how this is an important way of putting yourself out there, as well as forming the right relationships that will help you succeed. We saw how influencing and empowering others are skills we must develop as we journey to our life's goals, and we concluded with gratitude and how being in that place of gratitude puts you in a position to always attract what you need to achieve your goals.

What has the journey through these pages been like for you? I believe you have been introduced to a world of opportunities. I believe you have gained very important knowledge and have become more confident, about reaching your goals. Reading this book is your first step to fulfilling one of the many requirements of reaching your goals. The next step will require your action.

One of the reasons why many training programmes are not as successful in transforming people is that they focus on deploying information, which is good because you need the information to act upon but merely reading a book will not help you if you do not take any action. You have not read this far to refuse to act.

I will encourage you to go over the reflection questions and sit with them. Each one of those questions requires you to be completely honest with yourself about where you are on this journey to greatness. Answer them truthfully and be sure to complete the tasks. It is important to note that change is not easy and is not necessarily pleasant, and that is why many people never take that first step or they start with a lot of excitement and fall off along the way. I believe you are the kind of person who finishes what you start, these are the people who reach their goals, who make an impact and who succeed.

What is it going to be like for you? Are you committed to doing all it takes to succeed? I believe your answer is Yes! I am rooting for you and I wish you all the best!

Printed in Great Britain
by Amazon

39350868R00096